GUIDELINES FOR
CONTEMPORARY CATHOLICS
The Historical Jesus

GUIDELINES FOR CONTEMPORARY CATHOLICS:
The Historical Jesus

Michael L. Cook, S.J.

THE THOMAS MORE PRESS
Chicago, Illinois

ISBN 0-88347-188-4

The author wishes to acknowledge with gratitude permission to
incorporate passages of his own writing from:

THE JESUS OF FAITH: *A Study in Christology,* Copyright ©
1981 by Michael L. Cook. Reprinted by permission of the
publisher, Paulist Press.

"Jesus from the Other Side of History: Christology in Latin
America," by Michael L. Cook, from *Theological Studies.*

TABLE OF CONTENTS

FOR MOMMA
with love and gratitude

Publication of this book
is made possible in part
by a grant from
ANDREW M. GREELEY

I. INTRODUCTION

JESUS, during his historical ministry, was sent only to the lost sheep of the house of Israel (Matt. 15:24). His mission was to be a prophet to his people, a conscience calling them to the truest and deepest realization of their traditions. A prophet does not predict the future in any literalist sense. Rather, s/he employs powerful symbols, both in word and in deed, which capture the imagination and evoke deeply felt responses in the unconscious as well as the conscious experience of the people. In a word, the prophet opens up the possibility of a future that is new and creative by enabling people to appropriate their past in unforeseen ways. For the prophet, and so for Jesus, it is truly imagination that saves us, that is, the ability to perceive new and fresh possibilities in all the varied relationships that constitute our lives.

The primary symbol, or root metaphor, that Jesus employed with great effect was the Kingdom of God. What Jesus meant by this symbol, which was fraught with so many diverse expectations among his people, was unique to him. The scholarly debate as to whether he understood it to be simply future or simply present in his ministry misses the point. The future Kingdom will only come through an authentic and profound appropriation of the past that brings the reality of the Kingdom into the present and so opens up the possibility of a true future. Jesus was asked when the Kingdom of God was coming (Luke 17:20), and he replied that it was not coming with signs to be observed nor would they say "Lo, here!" or "Lo, there!" for "behold, the Kingdom of God is in your midst." What Jesus was saying, in effect, was that if you

9

are looking for your salvation to come through some outside intervention, whether that be the more esoteric expectation of God acting from outside in an apocalyptic manner ("signs to be observed") to destroy the present evil age, or the more popular expectation of God acting through a warrior hero from the house of David who would usher in the messianic age ("Lo, here—Lo, there") by destroying the enemies of Israel, the hated Romans, then you are looking in the wrong place. God is already acting in the midst of your lives, in all the complex relationships that constitute your personal and collective history. Jesus called his contemporaries not to look away from their lives for some outside intervention that would save them but to look ever more deeply *into* their lives and there discover the God who is already acting to save them.

This God seeks to liberate us from the power of evil that keeps us captive, which Jesus identifies as the symbolic power of his healing ministry (Luke 11:20 par.). Above all, this God seeks to liberate us from the evil we do to one another by our self-righteous attitudes that breed exclusivity and oppression. Jesus cries out victoriously in the face of the violence of those who oppose his proclamation of the Kingdom that the very ones whom they call "violent intruders" (Matt. 11:12 par.), i.e., the poor, the marginalized, the outsiders, are the ones who are "grasping" the Kingdom. The tax collectors and the prostitutes are entering the Kingdom of God ahead of them (Matt. 21:31) for they are open to the free gift of a gracious God. Finally, and most profoundly, that gift is identified as God's intention from the beginning of creation: the image of God as male and female (Mark 10:6 par.) which challenged their "hardness of heart" in a practice of divorce that was oppressive to women. He grounded the whole practice of the Law in the attitudes of the heart, whether that involved questions of murder, adultery, divorce, the taking of oaths, retaliation, or dividing the world into "neighbors" and "enemies" (Matt. 5:21-48 par.). In this, Jesus was simply calling his contemporaries to realize what was the true depth of their own heritage, namely that the whole Law is encapsulated in the final commandment of the heart: "Thou shalt not covet." But, in doing so, he was issuing a formidable and radical call to change their hearts and minds and to discover the God who saves in the very center of their lives.

As a prophet, Jesus was also a poet. The most striking way in which he sought to communicate what he understood by the Kingdom of God was in telling stories. Parables are metaphors in story form. As metaphors, they are not merely illustrative or informative, vehicles for understanding the less familiar by the more familiar (as in similes), so that once the "point" is understood the parable can be replaced by a clear and distinct proposition. As metaphors, they call for participation. One must "enter into" the parabolic world of Jesus in order to enter into the Kingdom. Jesus creates the Kingdom when he says that the Kingdom of God *is* a man sowing seed in a field. . . The parable does not exhaust the reality of the Kingdom but the Kingdom of God *is* this reality, i.e., the world in which we live seen now through the eyes of Jesus' creative imagination. Jesus does not create fables or legends with purely mythical creatures. He talks about the ordinary, everyday experiences of his contemporaries. Yet, his parables turn upon the possibility of seeing that familiar world in new and unforeseen ways. Finally, in his parables, Jesus does

not tell people what to do. If they truly enter into his parabolic world, they will know what to do.

The Good Samaritan (Luke 10:30-36) illustrates well the
approach of Jesus. He tells a story that would have been
very familiar to his listeners: a man traveling from Jerusalem to Jericho who is attacked by robbers, stripped,
beaten, and left half-dead. As a good storyteller, Jesus
draws his listeners into the story. What now will happen to
this poor man lying by the side of the road? As the priest
and Levite successively pass by, putting as much distance
between themselves and the poor man as possible, the
expectation of Jesus' listeners would have been for a good
layman, perhaps a Pharisee, to come along and help the
man. But, when Jesus says that "a certain Samaritan"
came along and then goes on to describe his actions in
terms of unheard-of generosity, an unexpected and indeed
unwanted element has been introduced into the story. The
ground has shifted, the familiar has become unfamiliar.
For, to Jesus' listeners, there was no such thing as a
"good" Samaritan. Samaritans were ignorant, backwater
heretics who did not believe in the whole Law. Jesus' description raises a question that many did not want to face:
can I conceive of a Samaritan acting in this manner? Can I
view a Samaritan as my neighbor? Jesus, as it were, held a
mirror up to his contemporaries and forced them to take a
hard look at their presuppositions and prejudices. He
called into question a whole mind-set that had categorized
a group of people as "outsiders." He gave a human face to
their enemies. And he told them, in effect, that they will
never enter into the Kingdom of God unless and until they
enter into this new way of "seeing" their neighbor.

It is not by looking away from our lives in all their relationships but only by entering ever more deeply into all

that makes us human that we will discover the God who saves already acting at the very center of those relationships. This is most poignantly communicated in Jesus' parable of the Prodigal Son (Luke 15:11-32). The Prodigal Son is not originally an allegory with the father representing God and the two sons representing respectively repentant Israel and self-righteous Israel, although the parable can be *used* in this way. It is rather a story about how fathers treat sons and sons treat fathers. The elder son was correct, according to the expectations of the time, in his anger. The father should have considered his younger son as one dead to him and, at the least, should not have given him any favorable treatment. Jesus' description of the father as one who did not stand on his prerogatives and did not insist on the hurt his son had caused him, but rather seeing his son coming from afar ran out and embraced him and kissed him, put the robe on his shoulders, a ring on his finger, shoes on his feet, and killed the fatted calf to celebrate, was certainly a shock to the imagination of his listeners: should a father love his sons in such a total and unconditional way? The parent-child relationship constitutes us in our humanness in a way that no other relationship can. If we would call God father in any meaningful sense, if we would experience the loving generativity of the God Jesus called *Abba,* then we can only do so in and through our own experience of the parent-child relationship, healing what needs to be healed and learning to love as the prodigal father loved. The God who saves us is at the center of such relationships and can only be discovered there. God's love is mediated through human relationships, and that is why the commandment to love one another stands at the very center of the New Testament.

What I have just described is an historical assessment of

the ministry of Jesus. There is more, much more, that can be said about the historical Jesus (for a readable overview I would recommend either Bornkamm or Greeley or Nolan from the Suggested Readings). But, I would submit that what is described, with its striking emphasis upon the divine activity as mediated through human activity, is at the very center of Jesus' proclamation of the Kingdom of God. Yet, the attentive reader will have noticed that such a reconstruction does not square exactly with any of the four Gospels as we presently have them. What justifies New Testament scholars in attempting such reconstructions, and are such attempts acceptable within the current teaching and doctrine of the Roman Catholic Church? This book will address itself to such questions as these. It will not attempt to write a full account of what might be said about the historical Jesus, i.e., to describe the results of the historical-critical method in New Testament study. Rather, it will address itself primarily to the *legitimacy* of the quest for the historical Jesus. This will, of necessity, involve us in the threefold question of past, present, and future, i.e., of the history of the quest, of current Roman Catholic teaching and doctrine with regard to what has emerged from the quest, and of contemporary thinking and debate among theologians concerning the directions the quest is presently taking. The latter raises the question whether there might be a future for the historical Jesus.

II. TRADITION AND HISTORY: 1778–1962

THE quest for the historical Jesus is, for the most part, a modern question that has developed and flourished only during the nineteenth and twentieth centuries. The Enlightenment saw the rise of rationalism and, correspondingly, the beginnings of a critical approach to Scripture. While Christians had always wanted to know what the man Jesus was really like, they had consistently presupposed in the preceding history of the church that the Gospels give us absolutely reliable information about him. Paraphrasing and harmonizing the four Gospels was the essential task of New Testament Gospel study. The modern question of historicity, as posed in terms of critical methodology, was certainly not uppermost, if present in any form at all, in the minds of the New Testament authors. They were primarily concerned to present the early church's faith commitment to Jesus in the light of the resurrection, although such a concern certainly included some interest in the historical past. But, it is important to note at the outset that the modern quest is *our* question, no less legitimate for that. We bring to the texts questions and methods that were not of primary concern to the first century authors and indeed to most commentators on Scripture throughout the history of the church until the Enlightenment. This does not mean that we are in a better position than our forebears with regard to faith commitment, but it does mean that we are in a different situation that can and does affect our faith commitment. It also means that we know some things better because of the long and complex history of biblical criticism.

This review of the history of the modern quest can be

conveniently divided into three stages: 1) the Old Quest: 1778–1906; 2) critical revision after World War I: 1918–1953; 3) the New Quest: 1953–1962. This history is almost exclusively European and Protestant, more specifically German and Lutheran. All Christians stand deeply indebted to the often painstaking and always careful work of the scholars whose names will be cited. If there is any area of church life that is truly ecumenical, the study of Scripture is certainly the most fundamental and important. Here we meet on common ground, and here we must listen to every voice that can illumine our understanding of the nature of Scripture.

1) *The Old Quest:* 1778–1906

Albert Schweitzer has written the best and most readable survey of this period in his classic book, *The Quest of the Historical Jesus.* What follows is largely a summary of his treatment.

(a) *From Reimarus to Strauss:* 1778–1835

Hermann Samuel Reimarus (d. 1768) was a professor of oriental languages, not a theologian; he was an "outsider" whose seven "Fragments" (published posthumously by G.E. Lessing between 1774 and 1778) were filled with hatred for anything that smacked of "obscurantism," i.e., that allowed religion to hold sway over reason. His famous seventh fragment distinguished between the "aim" of Jesus, a Jewish political messiah who failed, and the "aim" of the disciples, who stole the corpse of Jesus and created the figure of the risen Christ in order to gain adherents and thus make a living. The thesis of Reimarus is not especially significant. The best refutation of it is still Maurice Goguel's ironic observation that one could let oneself be persecuted for an illusion, but not for a fraud.

What is important is that Reimarus was the first to perceive clearly that the Jesus of history is not simply the same as the Christ proclaimed in the Gospels and by the church. To the delight of rationalists everywhere he drove a wedge between history and dogma, but their enthusiasm was tempered by the threat he posed not only to dogma but to Jesus as well.

The ensuing period can best be characterized as an attempt to break loose from any ecclesiastical dogma and to get back to Jesus, the man from Nazareth, whose personality and religion were the decisive factors for the contemporary scene. This gave rise to a multitude of lives of Jesus which passed from the uncritical mixture of the natural and supernatural of the earlier rationalism, through the fancifully imaginative and fictitious earlier lives and the fully developed rationalism of H. E. G. Paulus, to the more sophisticated and tempered rationalism of Friedrich Schleiermacher, who is considered to be the father of modern Protestant theology. There are two outstanding features of this period: the concern to interpret the miracles as naturalistically as possible, some more and some less depending on how thoroughgoing the rationalism, and the tendency to see not so much the past as the present in the past. What Schweitzer says of the earlier period can be applied in varying degrees to the whole: "For it, the problem of the life of Jesus is solved the moment it succeeds in bringing Jesus near to its own time, in portraying Him as the great teacher of virtue, and showing that His teaching is identical with the intellectual truth which rationalism deifies" (p. 28).

(b) *From Strauss to Wrede:* 1835–1901

When David Friedrich Strauss published his *Life of Jesus* in 1835, the definitive break between the nineteenth

century and all preceding generations had truly been
accomplished. Strauss was a Hegelian who viewed the
supernaturalistic explanation of the events of the life of
Jesus as the thesis which the rationalistic explanation had
followed as the antithesis. The synthesis that Strauss now
proposed was the mythological interpretation. Myth is
simply the clothing in historic form of religious ideas. In
the case of Jesus, the important thing is not what we can
know of him on the historical or natural level, still less the
extraordinary claims made for him in the miracle accounts.
The first is not recoverable in the same way as previously
thought, for the supposition that the Gospels of Matthew
and John were eyewitness reports is no longer tenable, and
the second is not verifiable, for such accounts either violate
or ignore all laws of causality, succession, and psychology.
What is important is the religious idea embodied in the
myth, i.e., the "idea of Christ," of God-manhood. This is
the eternal reality in the person of Jesus. The extent to
which this idea was actually realized in the historical
person Jesus is in the last analysis indifferent. What counts
is that the idea has entered the common consciousness. Its
realization in every personality is the ultimate goal of
humanity.

However, the real time-bomb in Strauss' book was not
the theory about myth but the assertion that the Gospel
of John is inferior to the Synoptics as an historical source
because it is more strongly dominated than they by theological and apologetic interests. Strauss reversed the pre-
vailing supposition of the day, defended strongly by
Schleiermacher, that John was the most reliable historical
source. He opened anew the search for the earliest and
most reliable sources about Jesus which would be the
unshakable basis for discovering the historical Jesus. The

conviction continued that a biography of Jesus "as he really was" could be reconstructed, given the proper evaluation of the sources.

The Marcan hypothesis, established by Karl Lachmann in 1835, was further shaped with the hypothesis of another source (a sayings source common to Matthew and Luke) by Christian Hermann Weisse in 1838. What eventually came to be known as the two-source theory (Mark and Q: more scientifically established by H.J. Holtzmann in 1863 and still the most commonly accepted hypothesis to explain the main sources of Matthew and Luke) gave great hope to the historicist temper of the nineteenth century that here at last were the purest and most immediate documents to reveal the Jesus of history. Weisse, however, whom Schweitzer sees as the only conscious continuator of Strauss, set up a roadblock to the historical study by his rejection of eschatology in order to defend the "originality" of Jesus as one who transformed and spiritualized the eschatological ideas. In so doing, he paved the way for the subsequent "liberal" Lives of Jesus, which would hold sway until the work of Johannes Weiss on eschatology in 1892.

Bruno Bauer, just five years after Strauss' *Life,* began his penetrating criticism of the Gospel history. Because he was overshadowed by the furor raised over Strauss and was considered, particularly in his later extreme views, to be an eccentric, his insights into the problems of Gospel criticism (which led him to postulate an original evangelist who invented the history) would not bear fruit until half a century later (with Wrede). In the meantime, there were further imaginative Lives of Jesus, which sought to combine criticism with fiction and which received their best known expression in Ernest Renan's *Life of Jesus* (1863). Renan's book is considered to belong to the "liberal" approach,

along with the later work of Strauss and others. These
writers all tended to reject eschatology in favor of a "spiritualized" interpretation of Jesus' messiahship. For the
most part, they sought a mediating position between the
alternatives of either the Synoptics (Mark being prior) or
John. John remained such a strong influence because he fit
in best with their own tendencies to psychologize the life of
Jesus, using the plan of Mark, but the "spiritual" view of
John. The bankruptcy of such an approach resulted in the
definitive consensus, originally argued by Strauss, that
John could no longer be seriously considered as an historical source. This separation between the Synoptics and
John also paved the way for the full recognition of the
fundamentally eschatological character of Mark and
Matthew. For Schweitzer, this is the net result of the study
of the life of Jesus in the period after Strauss: *a priori*
natural psychology gave way to eschatology.

What Schweitzer calls the "consistent" treatment of
eschatology finally appeared in 1892 with Johannes Weiss.
Schweitzer hails his work as equal in epoch-making importance to Strauss' first *Life of Jesus* because he lays down
the third great alternative which the study of the life of
Jesus had to meet: first, historical vs. supernatural; then,
Synoptic vs. Johannine; now, eschatological vs. non-
eschatological. Schweitzer himself has no use for those
who would seek a compromise between such alternatives.
They hinder progress. This is particularly true of those
who would waffle on Jesus' concept of the Kingdom of
God by trying to combine a "spiritual" with an apocalyptic view.

By this time, source criticism had reached the solid consensus that John and the Synoptics must be considered
separately and that within the Synoptics there are two

primary sources: a primitive form of Mark and a collection of sayings called Q (German *Quelle* = source). Nonetheless, the debate over eschatology, whether Jesus was completely dominated by it or repudiated it and which presupposition best explains the connection of events, continued on. This is reflected, above all, in the discussions over the title "Son of Man" among Aramaic scholars. However that question (which is still a subject of intense investigation) may be resolved, it must be admitted that, as the nineteenth century drew to a close, all attempts to "modernize" Jesus, i.e., to create the historical Jesus in the image of modern (nineteenth century) "man" had utterly failed. George Tyrrell's verdict on Adolf von Harnack's famous Berlin lectures, *What Is Christianity?* (1900) applies *mutatis mutandis* to the general work of this period: "The Christ that Harnack sees, looking back through nineteen centuries of Catholic darkness, is only a reflection of a Liberal Protestant face seen at the bottom of a deep well." For Schweitzer, what is left is a choice between the complete skepticism of Bruno Bauer, which challenges without exception all the facts and connections of events asserted by Mark, and an acceptance of the whole Gospel as historical, including the supernatural elements which are essential to it, at the same time trying to explain why certain narratives (e.g., the Transfiguration) are so supernatural and what their historical basis is. Wilhelm Wrede opted for the first horn of the dilemma and Albert Schweitzer for the second.

(c) *Wrede and Schweitzer:* 1901–1906

Wrede's *The Messianic Secret in the Gospels* and Schweitzer's *The Messianic-Suffering Secret* appeared on the same day in 1901. Wrede's approach of literary criticism led him to "thoroughgoing skepticism"; Schweitzer's approach of historical criticism to "thoroughgoing eschatology." They agree in their rejection of the contemporary psychological approach. In terms of critical arguments and reconstruction, particularly the recognition that a dogmatic element, the Messianic Secret, had intruded itself into the life of Jesus, they are in close agreement. They differ, however, in their explanation of the source of this inconsistency. Schweitzer puts it in the typically German style of stark and irreconcilable alternatives:

> There is, on the one hand, the eschatological solution, which at one stroke raises the Marcan account as it stands, with all its disconnectedness and inconsistencies, into genuine history; and there is, on the other hand, the literary solution, which regards the incongruous dogmatic element as interpolated by the earliest Evangelist into the tradition and therefore strikes out the Messianic claim altogether from the historical Life of Jesus. (*Tertium non datur,* p. 335).

Wrede's lasting contribution lies in his demonstration that the Gospel of Mark, just as much as the other sources, is dominated by theological rather than historical interest. Hence, Mark too belongs to the history of dogma. With that, the death-knell of the nineteenth-century biographical quest had been sounded. Schweitzer criticizes Wrede because his theory of the Messianic Secret cannot consistently explain all the messianic elements in Mark, particularly the three facts of Peter's confession, the entry into Jerusalem, and the High Priest's knowledge of Jesus' Messiahship. He seeks to overcome such inconsistencies by maintaining that the secret in Mark has to do not so much with Jesus' Messiahship as with the broader eschatological world-view which saturated the atmosphere of Jesus' day and which is the dogmatic element that constituted the thinking of the historical Jesus himself.

According to Schweitzer, Jesus was obsessed with eschatology. He expected the end of the world to come during his lifetime and so he sent the disciples forth to proclaim it, expecting that the Son of Man would come before they had even gone through the towns of Israel (Matt. 10:23). But, he was wrong. The disciples returned and the end had not come, so Jesus had to readjust his thinking. He now realized that he would have to die in order to force the coming of God's Kingdom. He embraced the cross and died, a noble but mistaken eschatologist.

Schweitzer, who had excoriated so brilliantly and so sharply the wishful thinking of psychological reconstruction, ended by doing the very thing he most criticized. A further irony was that he felt he had put an end to any further interest in the historical Jesus. With his emphasis upon eschatology as the key to the historical Jesus, he thought he had once and for all consigned Jesus to his own times, an interesting anachronism who could not speak to our own day except as "a mighty spiritual force," as "One unknown." He little realized what a key and central concept eschatology would now become in theological discussion.

2) *Critical Revision After World War I:* 1918–1953

Gerhard Ebeling sets the scene: ". . . the consciousness of being unable simply to continue on the nineteenth century's line of theological development, and of being called to subject church and theology to a thoroughgoing critical revision that takes its bearings from the Reformation, is the basic tendency that has established itself since the end of the First World War with surprising speed and power of appeal" (*Word and Faith*, p. 23). Aside from the renewed interest in eschatology, which was the legacy of Schweitzer, there were two other major factors which contributed to this reaction: the rise of form criticism and a growing opposition to history in the name of faith.

(a) *The rise of form criticism.*

The outstanding achievement of the nineteenth century was the development of source criticism, but by definition it was limited to the documents at hand. The twentieth century asked the further question: can we get behind the written documents to a period of oral tradition (ca. 30–65 A.D.)?

Hermann Gunkel paved the way for New Testament form criticism with his work on Genesis (1901). He established the basic presuppositions of the method: that there is a preliterary, oral tradition prior to the written documents, that this tradition normally circulated by means of small, independent units (pericopes), and that these units could be classified according to their formal patterns as determined by the reasons (various needs within the community) for their preservation. This last indicates that a history of the tradition could be written which would reflect the developing "life-situations." In the New Testament three principal stages could now be distinguished: the "life-situation" of *Jesus* in his actual earthly ministry, of the *early communities* in their new understanding and preaching about Jesus after his death and resurrection, and of the *Gospels* in their actual stage of composition by the evangelists. Joseph Fitzmyer summarizes this last stage well:

> Pursuing a method and a goal peculiar to each, the evange-
> lists used the tradition which had grown up about him in
> the preaching of Stage II. But they *selected* material from
> it (sayings and parables, miracle-stories, pronouncement-
> stories, and stories about him, John the Baptist, and the
> apostles), *synthesized* it into their own literary composi-
> tions, *explicated* it by redactional modifications and addi-
> tions, and *fashioned* it all into a unique literary form that
> we call "Gospel," indeed, into the four accounts which we
> know as the canonical Gospels (*Catechism,* pp. 20-21).

It should be noted, however, that at this point in our history of biblical criticism, i.e., prior to the later development of redaction criticism, the evangelists were considered rather as collectors than as authors in their own right.

Karl Ludwig Schmidt began the form-critical era of the
New Testament with the publication in 1919 of his book,
The Framework of the History of Jesus. This was the final
blow to any attempt to construct the history of Jesus using
the sequence of Mark. Schmidt isolated the individual
units from the framework. He considered these individual
units (both sayings and narratives) to belong to the oldest
tradition about Jesus. There were some collections into
small groups of materials prior to the writing of the
Gospel, but they were very limited and the only true exception to the rule of no continuous, coherent narrative in the
earliest period was the passion narrative (which pre-dated
the Marcan account). The evangelist himself provided a
framework of connecting links and "bridge passages"
which reflected his own interests and those of the early
church (its life, its worship, its apologetic and missionary
concerns). What this means, in effect, is that *no biography*
of Jesus is possible, neither an external, chronological

sequence of events nor an internal, psychological development. The framework can tell us something about the life of the early church, but only the single episodes can tell us anything about the life of Jesus.

Martin Dibelius, whose book *The Form-history of the Gospel* also appeared in 1919, developed the tools of form criticism in order to penetrate more deeply into the oral tradition itself. His main focus was upon the narrative material of the Synoptics, which he classified according to the missionary activity and needs of the early church. Two of his principles became axiomatic for form criticism: that the Synoptics were not strictly literary works but popularizations, and that the evangelists were not true authors, but collectors and compilers. In 1939 he applied his form-critical method to the life of Jesus in his book, *Jesus.* He accepted the axiom that no biography was possible, but he placed great historical reliability on the earliest forms and so wrote a rather full and confident account of the earthly Jesus.

Rudolf Bultmann, considered by many to be the greatest New Testament exegete of the twentieth century, did the first study of the entire Synoptic tradition, both discourse and narrative material, in his book of 1921, *The History of the Synoptic Tradition.* He built upon the conclusions of Schmidt and Dibelius, but he used form criticism not simply as a means of literary classification of a developing tradition but as a basis for judgments of historicity. Unlike Dibelius, he is extremely skeptical about the historical reliability of the sources. He is skeptical, above all, of the narrative material. He does allow that many of the sayings of Jesus most probably go back to Jesus but we can never be absolutely sure.

Here one is confronted with the methodological problem created by form criticism's stress on the role of the early church in transmitting, shaping, and even creating material about Jesus. It is possible to cut away anything that originated in Greek-speaking Hellenistic Christianity and to get back to the Aramaic-speaking Palestinian church. It is further possible to distinguish different layers of the Palestinian material insofar as it reveals the special interests of the church at various stages of development, so that an oldest layer can more or less be determined. But, how do we know whether this oldest layer really goes back to Jesus or simply to the church at a level we can no longer trace? Thus, in the introduction to his book, *Jesus and the Word* (1926), which seeks to examine what can be known historically of the life of Jesus, he can say: "Whoever prefers to put the name of 'Jesus' always in quotation marks and let it stand as an abbreviation for the historical phenomenon with which we are concerned, is free to do so" (p. 14). That historical phenomenon is the complex of ideas in the oldest layer of the Synoptic tradition. Jesus has been named as the bearer of the message. Bultmann admits that there is an overwhelming probability that he really was, but we cannot know for sure and, in the final analysis, it makes no difference.

(b) *Opposition to history in the name of faith*

In 1918 Karl Barth published his famous commentary on Romans in which he emphasized the importance of the experiencing subject for exegesis. In the preface to the second edition (1921), he protested with a reformer's zeal the kind of sovereignty the nineteenth century had accorded to historical critical methodology. Such research is only a prelude to the essential task of interpretation, which is to expose the "Word in the words," the religious significance of the documents for us. "Historical" exegesis should give way to "theological" or "pneumatic" exegesis. The real historical Christ is, in fact, the biblical Christ of the New Testament. The New Testament alone grasps the secret, the reality to this man. There is no need to try to go behind the texts to find an objective reality. Historical science cannot "prove" the faith nor can it even attain to the full reality of past events, for they are much broader than the limited scope of scientific method. Thus, Barth can emphasize the importance of the man Jesus as he is given to us by the New Testament witnesses and, at the same time, question the results of scientific historical scholarship.

Bultmann was an early sympathizer and defender of Barth's negative verdict on the nineteenth-century quest. But, Barth issued a call to believe in certain events as historical fact that cannot be established by scientific method. Bultmann does not deny that such events are possible, but he is unwilling to assume the historical truth of an event which is only possible and cannot be established methodologically. Barth broadens the concept of history until it is correlative to the content of faith. Bultmann sharply and radically opposes history to faith.

The key to Bultmann's approach is his indifference to the concrete historical element in past events. Not only do our sources make it difficult, if not impossible, to get back to the historical Jesus, but more importantly it is theologically illegitimate to do so. To seek an historical basis for faith would be a betrayal of Luther's principle of justification by faith alone. Bultmann took from his teacher, Wilhelm Herrmann, an abiding desire to preserve the "unprovability" of faith (while rejecting Herrmann's attempt to go behind the kerygma and establish the "inner life" of Jesus as the absolutely convincing ground of faith). Herrmann was, at the turn of the century, the opponent of Martin Kaehler, whose book of 1892, *The So-Called Historical Jesus and the Historic, Biblical Christ,* is not even mentioned in Schweitzer's survey and was virtually ignored until Bultmann took it up and reformulated it. Like Barth, Kaehler attacked the pretentions of historical scholarship. He distinguished sharply between the *historisch,* the bare facts of the past, and the *geschichtlich,* that which possesses abiding significance. The Gospels are kerygmatic and confessional, written in the light of Easter, but they alone give us the real Christ, who is the preached Christ, the Christ of faith. It is via the kerygma that we come into touch with the "historic" (*geschichtlich*) in the sense of what really happened. For Kaehler, this is the reliable, authentic "image" of the historical Jesus, his impact upon posterity. Bultmann took from Kaehler his emphasis upon the Christ-kerygma, but he interpreted it as a radical call to faith, devoid of any this-worldly security and therefore opposed to any historical interest that would compete with faith. The Christ-event is *geschichtlich* (or *eschatologisch*) as happening here and now for me in the church's preaching insofar as the message confronts me and effects a change in my self-understanding. This viewpoint led Bultmann both to de-historicize and to de-mythologize the kerygma.

Bultmann is unwilling to disengage the Christ totally from history, but he reduces the history that we find in the kerygma to the *Dass,* the bare fact that Jesus lived and died on the cross. He thus rejects any attempt to reduce the existence of Jesus to a mere myth or the Christ to no more than

a universal idea. Beyond that, the earthly Jesus, whatever
we may learn about him from historical research, has no
significance for faith. Jesus is part of the history of
Judaism, not Christianity. His message belongs to the presuppositions of New Testament theology, along with such
things as messianic expectations and Hellenistic influences,
for Christianity began at Easter with the proclamation of
the saving significance of the cross, and its theologians are
Paul and John. The paradox of Christianity is that this
bare fact, the death of Jesus on the cross, should be the
occasion of God's decisive eschatological act in human history. It follows that the contemporary task is not to pursue
the phantom of the historical Jesus but to interpret the
kerygma. That leads to the necessity of demythologizing
the message and translating it into modern terms.

Bultmann's dependence on the existentialist philosophy
of Martin Heidegger is well known. From Heidegger he
draws his concept of "modern man," particularly the tran-
sition from inauthentic to authentic existence. This is the
hermeneutic tool that he uses to interpret the message of
the New Testament in order that the true stumbling-block
of the Gospel may strike home: not the obsolete mythological world-view of the New Testament, but the challenge to
decision contained in the proclamation of God's decisive
eschatological act in Jesus Christ.

The radical character of Bultmann's demythologizing
can only be understood in the light of the concept of
human existence that is operative in it. Authentic existence
demands the abandonment of all ties with the world. We
must stand in the splendid isolation of free personal decision over against the world. We must not allow ourselves
to be drawn into the illusory security of worldly objects
and worldly evidence, for in so doing we will lose ourselves

in what is impersonal and neutral. For Heidegger, we can save ourselves by our own self-affirmation. For Bultmann, authentic self-knowledge is only possible as a gift of God. But, unless Bultmann is to fall victim at this point to the accusation that he is reintroducing mythology, his concept of God must be as radically opposed to this world as Heidegger's concept of human existence (*Dasein*). That is why Bultmann extends the concept of myth to any use of imagery that expresses the "otherworldly" in terms of this world. Such imagery is guilty of objectifying God, of making God a piece of this world, one who "breaks into" the world, history, community. But this is precisely the arena of inauthenticity, of everything radically opposed to God, who in this respect is the "wholly Other," irreducible to the world of things or objects or even to human existence.

Human language, indeed any kind of humanism, is related to faith as Law to Gospel. This sounds strange when we realize that Barth accused Bultmann of reducing theology to anthropology by making the only possible divine event a phenomenon of the human consciousness. But the kind of human self-understanding that Bultmann sees actualized in the kerygma is discontinuous with the normal web of human relationships. The only proper way to speak of God is in terms of *my* existence in faith. Such "analogical" talk avoids the problem of myth, i.e., of God being involved in the world. From such a stance it becomes clear why the Christ of the kerygma must remain unworldly and nonhistorical. The transcendent Word must meet us not in the flesh but in opposition to and isolation from the world, history, and community. Thus, for Bultmann, to demythologize is to dehistoricize, to remove any semblance of worldly reality from the Christ-event. Furthermore, insofar as the kerygma names Jesus as its criterion and manifests an interest in the significance of his human and historical life for faith, the logic of Bultmann's position, as Fritz Buri has pointed out, would call not only for demythologizing and dehistoricizing, but for "dekerygmatizing" as well.

(c) *Continuing concern for the original quest*

The desire to establish the constitutive significance of Jesus for Christian faith has prompted a great variety of reactions and responses to Bultmann. Principally, there are those who seek, in somewhat modified form, to continue the original quest and those who seek, in terms of a new methodology, to advance a new quest. Before treating the new quest, we should mention briefly some representative figures who, in various ways, have continued the original quest.

In England, C. H. Dodd emphasized the importance of the primitive apostolic kerygma, especially as found in Acts and Paul, but against the form critics he wished to show that this kerygma contained at least an outline of the public ministry of Jesus. He agreed with the result of form criticism that a complete biography of Jesus is impossible, but he sought to demonstrate, especially from Mark, that a broad chronological outline of Jesus' ministry had been preserved. Aside from the difficulty of establishing the hypothetical outline from the text of Mark, the basic presupposition of such an approach is that the primitive community was interested in the same kind of historicity as a nineteenth-century historian.

Similarly, the British exegetes T. W. Manson and Vincent Taylor both accept the main outline of Mark. They represent a zealous defense of the essential historical trustworthiness of the Gospels over against the extremes of form criticism, although Taylor is much more willing to use form criticism as a "limited tool" for research. However, their preoccupation with the objective historical reconstruction of Jesus' ministry has tended to displace the priority of the Easter experience of the disciples. History has instead become the foundation of faith. On the other hand, the great champion of form criticism in British scholarship has been R. H. Lightfoot. The emphasis upon the early church led him to investigate the intention of the evangelists. In this he was a forerunner of redaction criticism.

In Germany, Ethelbert Stauffer attempted to establish "new sources," e.g., increased knowledge of Palestinian conditions, Jewish polemics, and Jewish apocalypticism, as a means of checking and clarifying the Gospels and thus of establishing the uninterpreted facts of Jesus' history "as it really happened." He has been severely criticized for attempting to revive the positivistic, nineteenth-century, quest while ignoring the intervening fifty years of progress in scholarship. The exegete who is widely regarded as the leading custodian of exacting historical, environmental, and philological research is Joachim Jeremias. His careful and detailed methodology represents the most permanent contribution of the original quest. Such methodology remains very much a part of the new quest. Jeremias sees it as a bulwark against the modernizing of Jesus. However, like the other scholars mentioned here, he has tended to give absolute priority to the earthly Jesus to the detriment of the Easter experience. The historical Jesus confronts us with "a unique claim to authority." He writes, "If with utmost discipline and conscientiousness we apply the critical resources at our disposal to the study of the historical Jesus, the final result is always the same: we find ourselves

confronted with God himself.'' Jesus and the kerygma are
inseparable, but unequal, for Jesus' message is the "call"
and the kerygma is the congregational "response." "The
call, not the response, is the decisive thing" (*The Problem,*
pp. 21, 23).

Besides those who have sought to continue the original
quest by a modified and refined use of historical critical
methodology, brief mention should be made of those who
advocate a "special" kind of history. Karl Barth has
already been mentioned as one who would distinguish
between what happened and what can be established by
scientific method. For him, sacred history cannot be
simply equated with profane history. God's acts are not
subject to human methods. The foremost proponent of a
"special" kind of history, commonly known as "salvation
history," is Oscar Cullmann, who views history as a series
of redemptive epochs with Christ as the midpoint of linear
time. This forms the framework of his Christology: Christ
exercising temporally successive functions in the history of
salvation, i.e., preexistent, earthly, present, and eschatological. Aside from the exegetical difficulties in establishing such a unitary understanding of time and history from
Scripture, the main criticism must remain whether such a
view corresponds in any way to what contemporary historians understand by history.

Finally, in Scandinavia, another group of Bultmann's
critics is represented by Harald Riesenfeld and Birger Ger-
hardsson. They emphasize the importance of sacred oral
tradition in the formation of the Gospels, but restrict it too
exclusively to rabbinic techniques. Jesus was a Jewish
rabbi who taught his disciples by fixed verbal formulae and
solemn symbolic actions, which they memorized. This view
relies too much on undocumented construction and has

not received widespread support, especially since it tends
to reduce the sources, and hence Jesus himself, to a kind of
scribal literalism.

3) *The New Quest:* 1953–1962

(a) *The springtime of a "new programme":* 1953–1959

Despite Bultmann's avowed skepticism regarding both
the possibility and the legitimacy of a quest for the historical Jesus, his two early works on the history of the Synoptic tradition and on Jesus reveal a rather painstaking effort
to establish historically the words and deeds of Jesus. The
most interesting reaction to Bultmann has come from
among his own pupils, who in the so-called "new quest"
see themselves as furthering precisely this tendency in Bultmann's own work.

The new quest began in 1953 with a paper by Ernst
Kaesemann entitled "The Problem of the Historical
Jesus." In this address to former students of Bultmann at
Marburg, he outlined some of the fundamental presuppositions. First of all, he admits that no life of Jesus, no
biography that would involve exterior chronological or
interior psychological development, is possible. On the
other hand, he refuses to allow this fact to lead to defeat-
ism and skepticism with regard to the earthly Jesus. There
are three reasons for this. First, it would overlook "the
fact that there are still pieces of the Synoptic tradition
which the historian has to acknowledge as authentic if he
wishes to remain an historian at all." In connection with
this, he proposes that the safest ground lies in what has
come to be known as the criterion of "dissimilarity" or
"distinctiveness," i.e., that whatever cannot be directly
derived from or attributed to late Judaism or primitive

Christianity has the greatest claim to being an authentic
word or deed of Jesus himself. Second, it would overlook
the danger of docetism. If there is no connection between
the exalted Lord and the earthly Jesus, then we are in
danger of committing ourselves to a mythological Lord.
Third, and this is the heart of the problem, it would overlook the intention of the evangelists in writing Gospels.
". . . the exalted Lord has almost entirely swallowed up the
image of the earthly Lord, and yet the community maintains the identity of the exalted Lord with the earthly."
This points to the crucial issue of the whole quest, which is
"the question of the continuity of the Gospel within the
discontinuity of the times and within the variation of the
kerygma" (*Essays,* p. 46).

In developing what is distinctive of Jesus, Kaesemann
focuses on the characteristic traits in his preaching which
stand out in relatively sharp relief and can therefore be
compared and contrasted with the message of primitive
Christianity. The Gospel, he says, cannot be anonymous,
for it is tied to the person of Jesus whose words manifest
an unparalleled and sovereign freedom over against both
Torah and Moses. In a word, he makes an unheard-of
claim to authority which only the Messiah could make.
This theme of Jesus' claim to authority, and the certainty
implied in it, has become one of the predominant motifs of
the new quest.

Another former student of Bultmann, Ernst Fuchs,
seeks to balance Kaesemann's emphasis upon Jesus' words
by a parallel emphasis upon his conduct. In fact, he gives a
certain priority to the conduct of Jesus for two reasons.
First, he feels that the Gospel reports of Jesus' activity
would have a greater claim to historicity because the primitive community would be less likely to change the deeds

than the words of Jesus. And secondly, a person's conduct is a more reliable indicator than words of who or what s/he is. This reflects the emphasis in the Gospels on *doing* the will of God. Thus, Fuchs sees Jesus' conduct as the real context or framework of his preaching. The deed *par excellence* of Jesus' ministry is his table fellowship with tax collectors and sinners. For Fuchs, what is distinctive and extraordinary is that here Jesus dares to act in the place of God. Once again we see an unheard-of claim to authority. Fuchs insists that a parable such as the Prodigal Son should not be taken too hastily as referring directly to God's conduct. Rather, Jesus is defending his own conduct. This means that the parable is drawn from Jesus' conduct, which thus remains the primary point of reference to interpret the parable. In this case Jesus' action of going out to sinners is identified with the action of the father in embracing his sinful son with total and unconditional love. Jesus' conduct clarifies the parable rather than the reverse.

The crucial, and at the same time most vulnerable, point in Fuchs's presentation is the claim that both the words and the deeds of Jesus are a call to decision which is "simply the echo of Jesus' own decision." It is on the basis of his own decision that we must understand him, and that includes his suffering and death. Fuchs denies that this is a psychologizing of Jesus, although Bultmann will later accuse him of it. For the new quest, contra Bultmann, such a view is simply affirming that the new possibility of existence which God offers us in the kerygma first found its concrete embodiment and verification in a unique way in the *person* of Jesus himself. What the kerygma does through proclamation is make this new possibility accessible to all in their own concrete situations. Again, it is a

question of *continuity*. James M. Robinson sums up:
"Fuchs has carried through with regard to Jesus' action
the same thesis which Kaesemann presented with regard to
his message: in the message and action of Jesus is implicit
an eschatological understanding of his person, which
becomes explicit in the kerygma of the primitive church"
(*New Quest,* p. 16).

Guenther Bornkamm, just thirty years after the appearance of Bultmann's *Jesus,* produced the first full-fledged
work on Jesus to result from the initiatives of Kaesemann
and Fuchs with his now classic *Jesus of Nazareth.* While
there are many similarities to Bultmann in outline and
results, there are as Robinson points out "distinctive divergences" which reflect the concerns of the new quest. The
first is that Bultmann pretty well limits his presentation to
Jesus' *word* whereas Bornkamm expands his horizon to
include the events of Jesus' life insofar as these are historically ascertainable. The importance of human encounter,
the impact Jesus had upon people, is thereby stressed. This
concern for the human personhood of Jesus is, of course,
inseparably connected with the dominant motif of his
authority, a motif which Bornkamm shares with all the
new questers. Thus, the second "divergence": whereas
Bultmann sees the message of Jesus as primarily future
oriented, Bornkamm lays primary emphasis upon the
"unmediated presence" of Jesus' words, appearance, and
action, although he still recognizes the tension between
present and future. Bultmann's strong distinction between
Jesus and Paul has now become for Bornkamm (following
Fuchs) the distinction between John the Baptist and Jesus.
A correlative to this immediacy of Jesus is the recognition
that, while Jesus made no direct messianic claims for himself, "the Messianic character of his being is contained

in his words and deeds and *in* the unmediatedness of his historic appearance" (*Jesus,* p. 178). Finally, the third "divergence" is a consequence of the other two: the emphasis upon historical encounter with Jesus as eschatological encounter with God means that the kerygma continues in Christological terms what was begun in Jesus himself. It is true that only the Easter faith could disclose the full messianic mystery of Jesus, but it is one and the same person who aroused messianic hopes in his earthly life and is now proclaimed as the exalted Lord.

It was the contribution of Hans Conzelmann to focus everything on the question of eschatology. Jesus' understanding of time has been a much debated and key issue of the new quest. Conzelmann's thesis is that the structure of Jesus' preaching concerning the Kingdom of God cannot tolerate a synthesis with the expectation of another figure, the Son of Man, who would bring eschatological fulfillment. The reason is that Jesus' imminent expectation is indissolubly connected with himself so that another figure coming from heaven to inaugurate the end would render many authentic sayings about his own role unintelligible. Jesus unites in his own person the notion of futurity, the Kingdom as still to come, and the notion of imminence, the proclamation of the Kingdom as already present in his words and deeds. An interim is of no positive significance for him. He is not concerned with temporal chronology but with the urgency of the present moment, the concrete situation of his hearers that involves them in existential decision. Conzelmann sees the development of apocalyptic in the early church as stimulated by the intensity of Jesus' imminent expectation, but more importantly as reflecting the need to interpret the church's changing experience in new and different situations. He did one of the first redac-

tion criticism studies of Luke's Gospel. For him, Luke
with his periodization of salvation history looking to a
distant apocalyptic end represents the culmination of this
Synoptic development. Luke's theology is a deliberate and
radical modification of Jesus' own eschatological perspective, and therefore secondary and erroneous, a distortion.
Obviously, he is in strong disagreement here with Oscar
Cullmann.

Conzelmann's book *Jesus* presents a rather positive synthesis of what we can know historically. He also points to
the key problem in any attempt at historical reconstruction, namely the question of Jesus' self-consciousness. He
maintains that Jesus does not represent the Kingdom in his
person but the proclamation of its imminence which cannot be divorced from his self-consciousness. Cosmology
(God's providence), eschatology (God's coming), and
ethics (God's will) find their inner unity not in some logical
connection between them but in Jesus' understanding of
himself as the agent of a direct confrontation with God.
This is an "indirect Christology" which depends upon
Jesus' presence. This cannot be simply taken over after
Jesus' death, since Easter enabled the early church to grasp
the "new form" of Jesus' presence. However, Conzelmann maintains that the direct Christology of the kerygma
still requires an historical exposition of Jesus' life and
preaching.

Herbert Braun, in his essay on "The Meaning of New
Testament Christology," replaces the question of historical continuity with the question of constancy. Anthropology (human self-understanding before God) is the constant
and Christology is the variable. Bultmann finds that he
may be the most consistent among the new questers, for he

limits material continuity to the message of Jesus and thereby does not become involved in the person. For Braun, the intention that lies behind the variations in terminology (as exemplified in Jesus, the Palestinian community, and the Hellenistic community) is to communicate one and the same *content:* the paradoxical unity of the radicalized Torah and a radicalized grace. This content is neither mediated historically nor reducible only to an idea. It is the self-understanding of faith, something which happens over and over in human history. Thus, Braun seeks to establish material continuity while denying historical continuity (an interesting reversal of Bultmann's position). What "happened" in and around Jesus happens in and around Paul and John. "Jesus desires to occur again and again." Continuity in terms of titles, or conceptions about the person of Jesus, is not possible. Nor is it possible that Jesus could have handed on to Paul or John the concepts they use. The variable Christological terminology stands in the way of that. Within the three circles of Jesus, Paul, and John, the same event simply occurs over and over, each time in the varied and typical terminology of the particular circle: a remarkable constancy in human self-understanding. They all teach the same thing about the human situation before God. The use of the name Jesus by Paul and John is not arbitrary, for he is the one who "triggered" this constantly recurring event.

Gerhard Ebeling, in contrast to Bultmann, who maintains the constitutive priority of the kerygma, and in contrast to Braun, who seems to level off the event to discrete moments, each of which is equally significant, stresses the constitutive priority of Jesus himself, who is the "hermeneutic key" to any subsequent Christology. He is in sub-

stantial agreement with the results of Bornkamm: that in
Jesus himself the reality of God was made present and that
the three elements which form the central chapters of
Bornkamm's book (the rule of God, the will of God, and
the call to discipleship) belong indisputably to the authentic Jesus. Ebeling's contribution to the discussion is his
insistence that everything is concentrated in Jesus' call to
faith. His favorite expression for Jesus is "witness of
faith." A true witness (or prophet) is one who identifies
himself or herself with the word and takes responsibility
for it, even to the point of giving one's own life. The
remarkable thing about Jesus is his certainty. He is "the
Word which brings certainty." This concentration on certainty in faith implies the total identification of "person"
and "work" which renders every other interest superfluous. "The encounter with Jesus as the witness of faith . . .
is without limitation an encounter with himself. For the
concentration on the coming to expression of faith—and
that alone!—is the ground of the unity of 'person' and
'work', but for that reason also the ground of the totality
of the encounter" (*Word and Faith,* p. 298).

Ebeling recognizes that God's eschatological action
in Jesus cannot be adequately explained in terms of the
earthly Jesus alone. It is the proclamation of Jesus' death
that frees his eschatological existence from spatial and
temporal limitations, so that now it becomes a possibility
for everyone in their situation. This means that the "witness of faith" became, through the resurrection, the "basis
of faith." As "basis" Jesus both stands over against all
believers and is inseparable from them. Faith must remain
rooted in Jesus, for he is the "linguistic event which is the
ground of the event of faith." Ebeling's whole approach to
the new quest insists that:

we can find entirely in Jesus himself, and not first in some sort of additional new happenings of a historical or supra-natural kind, the *ground* both of the fact that what came to expression in Jesus *continues* to come to expression and of the way in which it does so . . . the historical Jesus is the Jesus of faith. Faith's view of Jesus must therefore assert itself as a furtherance to the historical view of Jesus. For faith itself is the coming to its goal of what came to expression in Jesus. The man who believes is with the historical Jesus (*Word and Faith,* p. 298).

James M. Robinson gave the new quest its name in his programmatic essay, *A New Quest of the Historical Jesus.* He begins with a review of the consensus that had been reached by 1959: that the original quest was *impossible* because of the kerygmatic nature of the sources and *illegitimate* because of the "attempt to avoid the risk of faith by supplying objectively verified proof for its 'faith'" (p. 44).

The *possibility* of a new quest resides in "a new concept of history and the self." Modern historiography, while not denying the validity of "the objective, factual level upon which the nineteenth century operated" (names, places, dates, occurrences, sequences, causes, effects), focuses upon "a whole new dimension in the facts, a deeper and more central plane of meaning" (the distinctively human, creative, unique, purposeful, which distinguishes humans from nature) (p. 28). The task of history is to grasp the acts of intention and commitment in which the self actualizes itself, and hence to grasp the *selfhood* therein revealed. Such an approach is formally analogous to the kerygma's interest in Jesus' history and selfhood.

The *legitimacy* of a new quest derives from "man's quest for meaningful existence." This again is formally analogous to the kerygma's interest, which is not to prove

faith but to confront us with existential decision. The
evangelists themselves "undoubtedly insisted upon the relevance of history for faith" (pp. 77–78). Whereas the original quest tried to drive a wedge between the Jesus of history and the Christ of faith, the modern approach sees that
the one cannot be isolated or separated from the other.
Rather, it seeks to differentiate in order to mediate an
encounter with Jesus *distinct* from an encounter with the
kerygma. Demythologizing, as analyzed by Robinson, provides the impetus, for it focuses upon the claim that the
myth (or the transcendent truth) has happened within history. The necessity of a new quest arises from our situation
today, whereby we have been given in modern historiography a second avenue of access to Jesus besides the
kerygma. Like the original disciples, who had their factual
memory as well as their Easter faith, we are allowed today
to see "the flesh of the incarnation." To proclaim Jesus
"in the flesh" is to proclaim the meaningfulness of all
human life in the flesh. That concern of the kerygma nec-
essitates and hence legitimates a new quest. To establish a
continuity between Jesus and the kerygma is not to prove
the kerygma true, but rather to prove "that the existential
decision with regard to the *kerygma* is an existential decision with regard to Jesus," i.e., that the kerygma is faithful to Jesus when it identifies "its understanding of existence with *Jesus'* existence" (pp. 92, 94).

Robinson's own approach to "the solution of typical
problems" shows a striking similarity to the approach of
Herbert Braun. He maintains, like Braun, that if we oper-
ate below the terminological level, we discover an underlying unity of meaning. Thus he focuses on the *message* of
Jesus. The terminological difference is seen in the fact that

Jesus' message is eschatological while the kerygma is Christological. This even includes a doctrinal difference, but when one moves beyond this initial comparison to the deeper level of meaning, one finds an underlying similarity in such paradoxes as in death, life; in suffering, glory; in judgment, grace; in finitude, transcendence. "It is this existential meaning latent in Jesus' message which is constitutive of his selfhood, expresses itself in his action, and is finally codified in the Church's *kerygma*" (p. 123).

Robinson's interest in "Jesus' transcendental selfhood," manifest in his approval of Fuchs's analysis of the existential decision of Jesus, differentiates him from Braun. His use of the term "selfhood" pinpoints the central problem of a new quest. Bultmann himself warns that "self-understanding" must be distinguished from "self-consciousness," and he accuses Fuchs and Ebeling especially of confusing the two. Self-understanding refers, in this context, to the understanding of existence of which Jesus, in his words and deeds and even in his fate, was the bearer. Self-consciousness on the other hand refers to Jesus' own appropriation of that understanding, his own attitudes, the decisions which he himself made, all of which must be inferred from his words and deeds. Van Harvey criticizes Robinson sharply at this point for wanting to put the heaviest kind of historical assent on that which can least bear it. The most difficult and tenuous kind of historical judgment is that which tries to infer motives from one's actions and speech, and even worse, the self underlying those motives. It is even more difficult in the case of Jesus, for we have no writings from him, no chronology of his life, and hence no real way of knowing if he ever changed his mind. While Harvey's criticism is valid, it should be noted that the above distinction between self-understanding and self-consciousness can be made too rigid and artificial if it implies that words and deeds tell us nothing at all about the person who is speaking and acting. In fact, it is only through words and deeds that interpersonal relations are possible at all. Within the limitations this implies, the new quest has an interest in the *person* of Jesus which is both possible and legitimate.

Another central problem of a new quest, pointed out by Schubert Ogden and Van Harvey, is that the two avenues of access to Jesus, kerygmatic and historical, either demand an *a priori* reduction of history to the role of confirming faith or leave open the possibility that history could disprove faith. All new questers agree that history cannot prove faith, but it would seem that the second horn of the dilemma must be accepted in this sense, that a disparity between Jesus and the kerygma (while not necessarily disproving faith) would at least radically change the character of faith. If faith has misunderstood the historical Jesus, then it has lost its basis, or at least it would have an object different from the one it has always proclaimed. Is this not in fact what Bultmann has done by shifting the object of faith from Jesus to the kerygma?

In the German edition of his book (1960), Robinson significantly modified his treatment of Bultmann. He saw the difference between Bultmann and his pupils to be much greater than at first supposed and so dropped the heading, "Bultmann's Shift in Position." He also recognized a greater complexity in Bultmann's attitude to the new quest inasmuch as Bultmann had always admitted some kind of quest. And finally, he reduced some of the psychologizing elements in the English version in the light of Bultmann's criticisms. All of these modifications were the result of

Bultmann's reaction to the new quest, to which we now turn.

(b) *Bultmann's reaction:* 1959

In 1959 Bultmann delivered a lecture on "The Primitive Christian Kerygma and the Historical Jesus." This is his famous response to the new quest in which he seeks both to clarify his own position and to point out the weaknesses he sees in the approaches we have just analyzed.

He begins by distinguishing two questions which he feels are often confused: the question of historical (*historische*) continuity and the question of material (*sachliche*) continuity. The first concerns the mere fact (*Dass*) of Jesus; the second the what and how (*Was und Wie*), the content (*Inhalt*), the subject-matter (*Sache*). An answer to the first is not necessarily an answer to the second. In fact, that is precisely the problem: how the proclaimer became the one proclaimed, how Jesus who proclaimed the "subject-matter" of the Kingdom became, as the Christ, the "subject-matter" proclaimed.

On the level of historical continuity Bultmann has always held a continuity between the historical phenomenon which is Jesus and the historical phenomenon which is the primitive Christian proclamation. This is decisively *not* to hold a continuity between the historical Jesus and the Christ, for the Christ of the kerygma has nothing to do with any historical figure. It is, however, to hold the paradoxical assertion that an historical event is the eschatological event. "It is therefore obvious that the kerygma presupposes the historical Jesus, however much it may have mythologized him. Without him there would be no kerygma. To this extent the continuity is obvious" (p. 18). On this level, the "That" (*Dass*) alone is decisive. Bult-

mann appeals to Paul and John to demonstrate that we do
not need to go beyond the That. Yet, he recognizes two
types of attempts to do so.

The first attempt, exemplified especially by Paul Alt-
haus, seeks to extract from the Synoptics an "historical
picture of the person and activity of Jesus," not to be sure
in the manner of the former Life-of-Jesus research, but
within the more modest limits of contemporary methodology. Bultmann is willing to meet such attempts part way,
and indeed his sketch of Jesus' activity is very similar to
Bornkamm's and Conzelmann's. Most significant is the
fact that he unhesitatingly ascribes to Jesus himself "a prophetic consciousness, indeed, a 'consciousness of authority.'" But all of this reconstruction flounders at the
crucial point: "The greatest embarrassment to the attempt
to reconstruct a portrait of Jesus is the fact that we cannot
know how Jesus understood his end, his death" (p. 23).
For Bultmann, the possibility that Jesus broke down cannot be glossed over. If the assumption of this first attempt,
that a portrait of Jesus is necessary to understand and
accept the kerygma, is to mean anything at all, then Jesus'
own understanding of the supreme saving event is a *sine
qua non.* We do not know how Jesus understood his
death; we only know how the primitive Christian community understood it. At this point, Bultmann reintroduces
the theme of legitimation that derives from his Lutheran
stance of justification by faith alone. Even if it were possible to establish Jesus' understanding of his death, it
could not legitimate the kerygma which proclaims Jesus as
the Christ who died for us. It is the kerygma that legitimates Jesus' history, not the reverse. Anything else would
be a perversion of faith.

The second attempt, "the argument that in Jesus' word and deed the kerygma is already contained *in nuce,* that Jesus' preaching already has 'kerygmatic' character" (p. 27), is much more to Bultmann's liking, for he sees Jesus as "a prophet with an eschatological message." Insofar as Jesus understood himself in this way, Bultmann is even willing to say that his proclamation implied a Christology. He accepts the "claim to authority," the "immediacy" of Jesus, the call to decision over against the person of Jesus "as the bearer of the word of God," "the imminent breaking-in of the kingdom of God" as belonging to Jesus' own consciousness. It would seem that he has accepted the whole program of the new quest. Yet, he maintains that all these elements merely point to historical phenomena. "The argument that the kerygma goes back to the claim of Jesus contained in his activity does not yet demonstrate the material unity between the activity and preaching of Jesus and the kerygma." Jesus remains on the level of the historical; only the kerygma is the eschatological event which addresses all people everywhere. "The Christ of the kerygma has, as it were, displaced the historical Jesus and authoritatively addresses the hearer—every hearer" (p. 30). Even if it could be proved that Jesus understood himself as Messiah and demanded faith in himself, it would make no difference, for the Christological kerygma demands faith "of a totally different kind."

Underlying Bultmann's attitude is the conviction that purely historical reconstruction by any kind of historical-critical method is simply incapable of establishing continuity between Jesus and the Christ. All that historical-critical methods can give us is a knowledge of mere fact (*Dass*). At this point, he asks whether it can be carried further "by an

interpretation of history based on the historic (that is, on
the existential) encounter with history." This leads him
into an evaluation of the leading views of the new quest.
His strongest criticism is of Fuchs and Ebeling, whom he
accuses of "psychologizing" because they do not maintain
a sharp distinction between self-understanding and self-
consciousness. He finds them inconsistent, for although
they do not intend to construe Christian faith as personal
relationship to the historical Jesus, this is in fact what happens when they move beyond the understanding of existence which one can derive from Jesus' words and deeds
and speak of such things as Jesus' own faith and decision.
He finds fault with Bornkamm and Kaesemann because
they do not distinguish clearly between historical interest
and existential interpretation. He sees Braun's existential
interpretation as perhaps the most consistent because he
focuses upon the content of Jesus' words, as does Robinson, and does not confuse that with historical interest.
However, both err in their attempt to give equal value to
the historical Jesus and to the kerygma, for it is *only* in the
kerygma that "the paradox 'in death life resides' first
became explicit." That is, a genuine existential dialectic is
not present in the formal pattern of Jesus' message, but
only in Paul and John.

What Bultmann is saying, in effect, is that there is *only
one* significant avenue of access to Jesus, and that is the
kerygma's proclamation of him as the Christ. It is the
kerygma that has changed the "once" of the historical
Jesus into the "once-for-all." This explains why Paul and
John can totally disregard any simple repetition of Jesus'
proclamation. If the historical Jesus could place the hearer
before a decision independently of the kerygma, then the

Christ-kerygma would have become superfluous and unnecessary. On the other hand:

> If it is true that the kerygma proclaims Jesus as the Christ, as the eschatological event, if it claims that Christ is present in it, then it has put itself in the place of the historical Jesus; it represents him. Then there is no faith in Christ which would not also be faith in the church as the bearer of the kerygma; that is, using the terminology of dogmatics, faith in the Holy Ghost. But faith in the church is at the same time faith in Jesus Christ, a faith which the historical Jesus did not demand (p. 41).

(c) *Realignments:* 1960–1962

Both Robinson and Ebeling have sought to answer Bultmann directly. Robinson's modifications in the German edition of his book have already been noted. His full-scale answer appeared in his article, "The Recent Debate on the 'New Quest.'" He begins by attacking caricatures of the new quest that had arisen, especially the continuing attempt to prove one's faith. The real motive of the new quest is not legitimation but understanding (*fides quaerens intellectum*). He then turns to Bultmann's article.

In response to Bultmann's analysis of the first attempt to go beyond the That, Robinson maintains that "Jesus' relation to his death is theologically relevant at only one point: When the kerygma speaks of Jesus giving up his life and accepting his death, is this talk about Jesus of Nazareth or, despite the use of his name, talk not about him but about, e.g., a non-historical death-resurrection myth?" (p. 202). What emerges is not Jesus' self-consciousness, but an understanding of existence implicit in the whole of

Jesus' life, including his death, and made explicit in the kerygma.

The further problem of the legitimate use of the Synoptics raises the crucial question of the nature of the Gospel form. Robinson proposes Conzelmann's theory that Mark was written to control and correct an excessive misuse of the Jesus-tradition, especially the excesses of the "divine man" Christologies. He suggests that our situation today is much like that of the evangelists, hence the necessity of a new quest. It is not enough to say that the kerygma legitimates Jesus' history. For, Jesus' history is also needed to legitimate the kerygma.

In response to Bultmann's analysis of the second attempt, Robinson claims no difference between Bultmann and himself on the question of Jesus' self-understanding, for he agrees that self-understanding does not necessarily emerge into self-consciousness. The real issue between them is where one places God's eschatological action. The issue clarifies when one recognizes that the problem of our present relation to Jesus' message is no different from our present relation to primitive Christianity's message. Both are in need of historical-critical and existential exegesis. It is arbitrary to affirm that of the New Testament text and to deny it of Jesus.

The general lines of Robinson's reply correspond closely to what Ebeling says in his book, *Theology and Proclamation*. The fundamental problem is again where one places God's eschatological action. Is the constitutive event of Christianity to be placed primarily in the kerygma of the primitive church or in Jesus himself?

Ebeling insists on the validity of the new quest, on the unavoidable need to "get back behind the kerygma," not

to provide legitimation for it but an interpretation of it.
The kerygma not only illumines our self-understanding, as
Bultmann would have it; it also illumines what has happened. And what has happened, in turn, illumines the
kerygma. Both ways of interpretation are complementary.
The need to find the "hermeneutic key to Christology" is
the decisive driving force behind the new quest.

In response to Bultmann's objection that the new quest
would render the kerygma superfluous, Ebeling proposes
"two very closely connected theological reasons" for the
"theological necessity" of the quest. First, the kerygma
itself speaks of Jesus as an historical person. That this is
theological is based on Ebeling's view that to think consci-
entiously as a theologian today is to think historically. And
second, if the Christ of the kerygma has really "crowded
out the historical Jesus," then Jesus himself would have no
more importance to the understanding of the kerygma
than that of a "random and meaningless cipher." The
common element in all the variability of the kerygma is
"the proclamation of the name of Jesus." "The kerygma
itself names Jesus as its criterion." In sum, if the real
intention and concern of the kerygma is not to contradict
Jesus but to correspond to him, to let him alone count,
then it is of vital concern to discern the identity and the
difference between Jesus himself and the statements of the
kerygma about him.

Bultmann's own terminology of implicit and explicit
Christology should force him into asserting the "material
unity of the ministry and preaching of Jesus with the
kerygma." Ebeling sees part of the reason for their disagreement to lie in "a confusion about the meaning of the
phrase 'the mere That.'" There is a basic ambiguity in

Bultmann's use of it: "The confusing thing here is that on
the one hand the concept of the That is charged with the
greatest possible meaning as the eschatological call to decision—we can now add: of the Word of God—which takes
place here and now; on the other hand it is emptied of all
meaning as the mere historicity of the person of Jesus"
(p. 72). Ebeling says that all may still be well if it is recognized that for God's Word the That and the What are identical as the pure, authoritative Word which creates faith.
But that applies equally to Jesus and to the kerygma.
Hence, the task of interpretation, *pace* Bultmann, is to
examine the proclamation and activity of Jesus, and then
to show how the kerygma as Word of God depends on its
invocation of the name of Jesus.

Ebeling concludes this section with Robinson's point
about our present relation to the past: if the self-understanding of the kerygma can be handed on as eschatological event, why not the self-understanding of Jesus? Both
are historical phenomena which are open to historical-
critical and existential interpretation. Moreover, as previously noted, Ebeling maintains the constitutive priority
of Jesus. It is this event alone—Jesus, the Word of God, in
whom God came, who has made God intelligible to us and
who in turn claims our obedience—"which legitimates the
homological form of explicit Christology" (p. 78).

In an appendix entitled "Psychologizing interpretation
of Jesus?" Ebeling responds to Bultmann's main criticism
of himself and Fuchs. He maintains that it "would scarcely
be possible to banish psychological interpretation altogether from historical work." Our concern should be to set
the proper limits, "i.e., to limit it to the subject-matter of
psychology." He takes Bultmann to task for making a too

rigid and artificial distinction between the objective and subjective in matters of faith. This leads to a separation of person and subject-matter which renders the concept "witness of faith," and hence the concept of authority, meaningless. In matters of faith "the Word demands the identification of the person with the subject-matter." In the context of Jesus' own faith, Ebeling "intentionally did not speak of Jesus as a believer but as the witness of faith. This was to bring out unmistakably the fact that the relation between Jesus and faith is grounded in the word-event and points to the word-event; that is to say that faith is seen not as something which can be ascertained, or guessed at by inference, but as that which came to expression in Jesus." This corresponds to a favorite dictum of Bultmann's that "Jesus' person coincides with his Word." For Ebeling, that which has come to expression linguistically is ascertainable through historical methodology.

In conclusion, Fuchs and Ebeling emerge as the most outspoken advocates of the new quest, to the point that they are accused of reviving the nineteenth-century quest. Robinson tags their position as "neo-liberalism." This, plus Bultmann's reaction, has led Kaesemann and Conzelmann to be much more reserved toward the quest. In fact, Conzelmann has withdrawn from it insofar as he regards Bultmann's reaction as an adequate statement of his own position. He now maintains with Bultmann that one is free to inquire after the historical Jesus but that such inquiry has no relevance for faith. Kaesemann, with his thesis that the apocalypticism of primitive Christianity was the matrix of Christian theology, has evoked strong opposition from Fuchs and Ebeling. Such a view places the beginnings of Christian theology *after* Jesus, thus destroying the thesis that Jesus as Word-event is the ground of faith and hence of all subsequent theologizing.

Carl Braaten, in his Preface to *The Historical Jesus and the Kerygmatic Christ,* can refer to the "winter of our discontent" and to the "end of the beginning" of the new quest. He sees the new quest as "a pause, as an experiment, on the way to refining and redefining a methodology which till now has challenged the unity of theological knowledge" (pp. 7, 11, 12). However, New Testament methodology has tended to move in other directions. Redaction criticism, with its emphasis upon the editing process in the Gospels and hence on the authorship of the evangelists, has moved to the forefront of biblical criticism. Again, former students of Bultmann have done the groundwork: Bornkamm on Matthew, Conzelmann on Luke, and Willi Marxsen on Mark. From the early sixties, the focus of interest in biblical studies has been primarily upon the text itself: the composition as a whole (redaction and composition criticism), the use of literary genres and techniques (literary criticism), the audience for which it was intended (audience criticism), the impact upon different historical and cultural epochs (the hermeneutical circle), and most recently the social context (including description and analysis as well as the application of various theories).

Nonetheless, the quest of the historical Jesus, while it peaked in the late fifties, has continued to attract scholarly interest and, perhaps more importantly, has found its way into the popular consciousness. This is particularly true within Roman Catholicism since Vatican II, and nowhere has the historical Jesus been more strongly emphasized than in that movement, uniquely rooted in the Roman

Catholic experience, known as liberation theology. To understand this development, we must first examine the official teaching of the church as it relates to the history of the quest within Protestantism and then return to the thinking and debate of the past twenty years in order to ask what might be an acceptable position for Catholics today.

III. CURRENT TEACHING AND DOCTRINE: 1943–1965

THE pre-Vatican II generation of Catholics will remember the popularly held belief that the Bible was the Protestants' book while the Catholics had the sacraments. If we needed to know what was in Scripture, the church would interpret it for us. In the opinion of this writer, the single most important factor that led to the phenomenon we now know as Vatican II was the official recognition of the validity of critical methods developed by Protestant scholarship in the nineteenth and twentieth centuries, and the encouragement given to Catholic scholars to employ these methods. This, it seems to me, is both cause and effect of the ecumenical movement which has broken down many of the stereotypes and barriers to communication in the past. The Word of God, sacramentalized in both written text and enacted ritual but ever again breaking through into new possibilities in the living voice of all ecclesial communities, has been our common meeting ground.

But, for Catholics, the path to this acceptance and appropriation of contemporary biblical methods was slow and arduous. In 1902 Pope Leo XIII did establish the Pontifical Biblical Commission, but given the temper of the times and the reaction against Modernism, its role, especially under Pope Pius X, was more that of guarding against false interpretations, principally by answering questions in the form of *responsa*. The fourteen given between 1905 and 1915 set a tone of reactionary conservatism that greatly hindered the development of Roman Catholic biblical scholarship until Pius XII's famous encyclical of 1943, *Divino Afflante Spiritu*. What follows is a brief summary of the three most important documents of the magisterium with regard to biblical studies: a papal encyclical, an instruction of the Biblical Commission, and a conciliar statement. (For a fuller and more nuanced account, see the appendix to Joseph Fitzmyer's *Christological Catechism*, pp. 95–142). Taken together, these three documents have had an impact on Catholic biblical scholarship that is nothing short of revolutionary.

1) *Divino Afflante Spiritu:* 1943

This encyclical, written on the occasion of the golden jubilee of Leo XIII's *Providentissimus Deus* (1893), marks the most significant turning point in the history of Catholic biblical scholarship, for in principle it recognized the validity of contemporary methods. Leo XIII had already affirmed that the whole of Scripture is inspired and that the human authors have written down everything and only those things which the Holy Spirit wanted, namely those truths necessary for *salvation,* an emphasis repeated at Vatican II (see *Dei Verbum,* par. 11). What Pius XII recognized was that the conditions for biblical study had been dramatically changed by discoveries in the fields of archaeology, ancient languages, and newly discovered manuscripts which were throwing new light particularly upon the *literary forms* used in biblical times. Thus, he encouraged Catholic biblical scholars to know the ancient languages, to seek to establish through textual criticism the best original text (alongside the Latin Vulgate), and above all to interpret the sacred text by expounding its *literal* sense. To do this they must draw not only on the wisdom of the earlier Fathers and Doctors of the church but employ the methods of modern criticism as well. Pius XII put particular emphasis upon the human author through

whom the divine communication takes place. This
demands special attention in exegesis both to the *intention*
of the human author and to the variety of *literary forms* in
which the divine truth has been expressed. These two
points are also included in Vatican II's document on revelation (see *Dei Verbum,* par. 12).

For Catholic biblical scholars, this encyclical amounted
to a mandate to employ fully and freely the critical methods that had been developing since the Enlightenment. As
Fitzmyer points out, the Biblical Commission began there-
after to play a more open-minded and positive role in pro-
moting Catholic biblical scholarship. In 1955 two secre-
taries of the commission published independently of one
another a significant distinction between those decrees of
the Biblical Commission that touched on faith and morals
and those that dealt with literary criticism, authorship, etc.
—the latter being most of the decrees issued between 1905
and 1915. "The former were to be understood as still valid;
the latter were to be regarded as time-conditioned and cor-
responding to an historical context no longer existent"
(Fitzmyer, *Catechism,* p. 99). Catholic scholars could pursue matters touching the latter "with full freedom." This
new freedom culminated in the commission's own
"Instruction on the Historical Truth of the Gospels."

2) *Sancta Mater Ecclesia:* 1964

This document strongly and openly affirmed biblical
criticism and made unhesitating use of the threefold stages
that resulted from form-critical analysis, namely the three
"life-situations" of Jesus' ministry, of the apostles'
preaching, and of the evangelists' writing. Although it was
entitled "An Instruction on the *Historical* Truth of the

Gospels," the emphasis is not on historical but on *truth,* as Fitzmyer demonstrates (pp. 105–106).

The Instruction is primarily aimed at exegetes, though other interested parties are addressed. The tenor is positive as the introductory paragraphs recognize the achievements of the past, the continuing difficulties encountered in doing solid exegesis, and the need to forge ahead for the good of the church. In its directives to exegetes the document explicitly affirms both the form-critical and the redaction-critical methods, while clearly differentiating the use of such methods from "the prejudiced views of rationalism." These views, which have intruded into the modern quest, as we have seen in chapter two, can lead to such excesses as an *a priori* denial of "strict revelation," a complete separation of faith and "historical truth" (this is the only use of the adjective "historical" in the text), and on overemphasis upon the "creative power" of the early community (par. V). One hears strong echoes of Bultmann in this paragraph.

While such a caution is well taken, what is of greatest significance is the positive acceptance and use of the three-fold distinction that has resulted from the above methods. This means, in essence, that one cannot simply identify the stage of Jesus' own ministry with the stage of Gospel redaction and final composition. Any form of naive fundamentalism is ruled out. A processive movement from the time of Jesus through the apostolic preaching of the early church to the final redactional use of their sources by the evangelists is taken for granted. While there is continuity from one stage to the next, one cannot assume absolute identity. Thus, as Fitzmyer explains so well, the inspiration of Scripture guarantees "Gospel-truth," not historical truth (pp. 117–118, 128). The Instruction concludes its treatment of the three stages this way:

> Unless the exegete pays attention to all these things which pertain to the origin and composition of the Gospels and makes *proper use of all the laudable achievements of recent research,* he will not fulfill his task of probing into what the sacred writers intended and what they really said. From the results of the new investigations it is apparent that the doctrine and the life of Jesus were not simply reported for the sole purpose of being remembered, but were "preached" so as to offer the Church a basis of faith and morals (par. X, trans. Fitzmyer, ital. mine).

Fitzmyer notes some unresolved problems that the document does not treat, e.g., the relationship of the Synoptic Gospels to one another, the reinterpretation of the actual words of Jesus in the compositions of the evangelists, and the historicity of the infancy narratives. Instead, the Instruction concludes its directives to exegetes: "There are still many things, and of the greatest importance, in the discussion and explanation of which the Catholic exegete *can and must freely exercise his skill and genius* so that each may contribute his part to the advantage of all, to the continued progress of sacred doctrine, to the preparation and further support of the judgment to be exercised by the ecclesiastical magisterium, and to the defense and honor of the Church" (par. XI, trans. Fitzmyer, ital. mine). This is almost a direct quotation from Pius XII's *Divino Afflante Spiritu* (par. 49), with the significant addition of the phrase referring to the magisterium of the church. The Catholic biblical scholar must never forget that his or her work is always in service to the church as a whole. Yet, s/he must freely exercise all the skill and genius available in the continuing quest for a deeper understanding and explanation of such biblical problems.

3) *Dei Verbum:* 1965

Vatican II's *Constitution on Divine Revelation,* though one of the first proposed in 1962, was one of the last approved in 1965 as it went through many drafts and revisions. It is significant that the Biblical Commission's Instruction appeared during the course of this debate and even more significant that it was recapitulated in paragraph 19 of the Constitution. Thus, the highest authority in the church effectively made the Instruction its own (Fitzmyer, pp. 21–22).

In the course of the summary paragraph 19, the Council refers to the church's constant assertion of the "historical character" of the four Gospels, but then goes on to describe that historical character in the language of the Instruction.

> The sacred authors, however, wrote the four Gospels, selecting some things from the many which had been handed on either by word of mouth or in writing, reducing some of them to a synthesis, explicating [*explanantes* (see Instruction, par. IX)] some things in view of the situation of their churches, and preserving the form of proclamation but always in such fashion that they recounted to us the honest truth about Jesus [vera et sincera de Jesu]. (trans. Fitzmyer)

By using the words *vera et sincera* (= "honest truth"), the Council rejected a proposal to make true and historical simply equivalent (Fitzmyer, pp. 124, n. 41 and 141–142,

nn. 3 and 4). The summary reflects the struggle that went
on during the debates but, in the final analysis, it firmly
places the church's magisterium on the side of the new
directions in biblical criticism. This is not to say that every
new development in biblical criticism is simply accepted
without question. Biblical scholars themselves disagree
about many interpretations and through open and scholarly debate seek to provide a corrective to extremes. But it
does mean that the three documents just analyzed as reflecting the current teaching and doctrine of the magisterium do accept in principle contemporary biblical methods. However any particular issue in biblical studies may
be decided, the point is that we live for better or for worse
in the age of biblical criticism. The tide of history cannot
be reversed.

Where, then, does that leave us with regard to the historical Jesus? This should be seen as a question of both faith
and praxis, i.e., of what we believe and of how we live it.
What is the relationship between faith and history, between the Christ of faith and the Jesus of history, and how
does knowledge of the historical Jesus affect our lives? In
the light of the history of the quest and of the current
teaching and doctrine of the magisterium, these are the
continuing questions that frame the contemporary thinking and debate.

IV. CONTEMPORARY THINKING AND DEBATE: 1965-1985

MOST of us, unwitting children of the Enlightenment with its rationalist and historicist tendencies, probably subscribe to the following proposition: "If it didn't happen, it isn't true." To identify truth *only* with what can be experimentally described or defined through scientific, historical, or philosophical reason is so much a part of the furniture of our modern minds that we are scarcely aware of it. But mystery, the deepest truths of the human condition, cannot be reduced simply and unequivocally to the descriptions and definitions of historical or abstract truth. Such language, products of finite human minds at least one step removed from the actual complex pluralism of lived reality, is always derivative, secondary. Mystery cannot be simply described or positively defined. As Avery Dulles has pointed out, it can only be "evoked." Only symbol, which embodies the whole of human experience in all its concreteness and diversity, has the power to evoke the mystery.

This is not to deny the importance and legitimacy of our descriptions and definitions, but it is to ask where they are to be located in reference to the mystery that is Jesus. The contemporary concern to understand and articulate the relationship between the Jesus of history and the Christ of faith, emerging as it does out of the whole preceding history of the quest, must of necessity engage the issue on both the theoretical and the practical level. Hence, this chapter will concentrate on each in turn: first, a theoretical "solution" coming primarily from the resources of Anglo America, and then a practical "application" from Latin America. Finally, we will propose a move toward a more synthetic view of the whole discussion in terms of the primary language of symbol, metaphor, and story.

1) *The importance of historical knowledge for faith: a theoretical "solution"*

The literature of the past twenty years relating to the quest of the historical Jesus, both Catholic and Protestant, suggests a consolidation of positions achieved rather than any new and creative breakthroughs. Although some reject the quest altogether, most scholars will admit that some knowledge of the historical Jesus is indeed possible within the limitations of the historical-critical method. Details may be debated, and a greater or lesser amount of material may be admitted as historical according to one's presuppositions (compare, for example, the books of Jeremias and Perrin), but there is a reasonably large and secure consensus on the essential elements of what can be said historically about Jesus. The books listed in the Suggested Reading reflect such a convergence on the possibility of the quest and its results.

The real issue today remains the one that Bultmann identified more than fifty years ago: not whether some historical knowledge of Jesus is *possible,* but whether it is *legitimate* given the nature of faith. The debate revolves around the question of knowledge: does faith give us a kind of knowledge that is independent of the contingencies of history? Or, is historical knowing the only way we know anything? If distinct, is there any relationship between historical knowledge and faith knowledge? *Sancta Mater Ecclesia,* in its only use of the adjective "historical," warns against "a false idea of faith" that would see faith as having nothing at all to do with historical truth. This seems aimed primarily at Bultmann.

However, there are at least three possible positions that one can take on the relationship between faith and history. The first sees history as absolutely constitutive, without remainder, of faith knowledge. This can take two forms: (1) a naive fundamentalism that simply equates every statement in the Bible with historical fact. The authority for such a view may be based simply in an appeal to the authority of the Bible itself or of church pronouncements or even of one's own subjective conviction. This approach, which in its variations can be identified with traditional belief, raises a problem not in its desire for certainty but in the falsifying influence that belief can have upon the critical ideal of assent in historical judgment. The very things that we might wish to believe most passionately as Christians, e.g., virginal conception, nature miracles, bodily resurrection, are precisely those things that can elicit little or no assent on the basis of critical historical method. (2) The second form is a more sophisticated historical confessionalism that will only admit to faith what can be established as historical through critical method (see the books of Jeremias and Harvey). This raises the same problem as above, but in reverse. Now the content of our faith is so reduced that it may no longer be in recognizable continuity with our past traditions, e.g., again in the understanding of virginal conception, nature miracles, and most importantly bodily resurrection. Insofar as these "events" cannot be established through historical method, they are marginalized for Christian self-identity and at best are retained as mythic expressions of a message that can be translated into contemporary terms.

The second position, which is that of Bultmann, maintains an absolute opposition between history and faith. Each belongs to its own separate sphere. History deals with

contingency and can give only relative certitude according
to the varying degrees of affirmation that range from mere
possibility to a high degree of probability. Faith, on the
other hand, is self-authenticating and so gives us a kind of
certitude that is independent of the vagaries of history.
Thus, the absolute quality of faith must in no way be dependent upon the relative, probability character of historical research. This, of course, raises the problem of
whether faith is related to history in any sense at all.
Although Bultmann insists on historical continuity in the
mere fact that Jesus lived and died on the cross, he effectively reduces Jesus to a random cipher, to no more than
an occasion for the divine activity. The logic of his position
is that the individual, historical person, Jesus in all his
concreteness and contingency, has nothing to do with
Christian faith. The problem does not lie in his understanding of history, which he shares with contemporary
historians, but in his notion of faith as absolutely independent of the historical. Indeed, does faith give us the kind of
absolute certitude that he supposes?

The third position, which is the one being proposed here
as a solution and which is closer to the thrust of the new
quest, seeks to mediate between simple identity and simple
dichotomy. It seeks to posit a necessary interaction and
interrelationship between history and faith. Faith must in
some sense be dependent upon historical knowledge. As
with the position of Bultmann, this approach recognizes
and accepts the tentative, probability character of historical judgment, but at the same time it affirms that faith
(while not simply to be equated with history) must be open
to all the ambiguities of history insofar as it is tied to a
concrete, contingent historical event (and person). Moreover, faith itself, by its very nature as the necessary and

appropriate stance for human beings in a world that is still moving toward its final consummation, does not give us absolute certitude but the kind of certainty that allows us to trust in a promised future. Faith itself is the risk, not in Bultmann's sense of a naked step into the abyss over against the human and historical, but in the sense of drawing us ever more deeply *into* the human and historical. Faith as the ability to trust constitutes us as human persons in the very historicality of our existence.

Norman Perrin, in the last chapter of his *Rediscovering the Teaching of Jesus* (1967), has offered a useful framework for working out the solution being proposed here (see my *Jesus of Faith,* pp. 22–27). Basically, he introduces a third dimension to Martin Kaehler's distinction between *der historische Jesus* (history) and *der geschichtliche Christus* (faith). There are three different kinds of knowledge. First, there is "historical knowledge," which is essentially descriptive. This is the kind of knowledge established by scientific methodology. It is "neutral" in the sense that it is open to any critical observer and is thus subject to revision. Second, there is "historic knowledge," which has two dimensions: the meaning a past event can have in its own context and the meaning it can have insofar as the past assumes direct significance for the present, i.e., speaks to our contemporary experience. While the distinction between fact (historical knowledge) and meaning (historic knowledge) is valid and necessary since there can be varieties of interpretations of the same fact, depending upon the perspective of the interpreter, still there can be no separation between them. Every fact is an interpreted fact. Moreover, the interpretations of our past traditions must always be in dialogical interaction with the interpretations of contemporary experience. Thus, fact and meaning belong together as part of the total historical phenomenon. As such, the phenomenon is open to any critical observer, whether s/he personally takes the same stance or not. The difficulty with Kaehler's original distinction above is that it tends to identify historic knowledge with faith knowledge, and thus reduces faith to a dimension of history, i.e., one among many possible perspectives on the same fact (this is Van Harvey's position in *The Historian and the Believer*).

Thus, Perrin clearly differentiates a third kind of knowledge which he calls "faith knowledge." This knowledge is different in kind from the first two distinctions, which belong within the purview of the historian's craft. Faith knowledge is not open to any neutral observer in the same sense (though as an historical phenomenon that has had effects within history it can be studied by historians), for it claims a different source, namely the divine activity. As such, it is transhistorical. Likewise, it is analogous to the fundamental human experience of mutual trust (I-Thou relationships) for, while the divine activity is the freely given origin (grace) that makes the relationship possible, it is in Christian terms an entrusting of oneself to Another (God as revealed in the person of Jesus). Finally, it may or may not be related to historical/historic knowledge.

Perrin sees this threefold distinction as a clarification of Bultmann's position, which he places in the center as over against those on the "right" (Jeremias), who tend to see historical knowledge as somehow directly constitutive of faith knowledge, and those on the "left" (Harvey), who tend in one way or another to reduce faith knowledge to historic knowledge. However, he seems to move beyond Bultmann and closer to the new quest insofar as he sees a positive, a negative, and a direct function that historical/historic knowledge can play in relation to faith knowledge.

The question, which would definitely contradict Bult-mann's position, is whether such a role for history is indispensable for faith.

Perrin affirms that as Christians our primary relationship to Jesus is one of faith. Each of us has a "faith-image" of Jesus which has grown out of the multivalent complexity of our human experience, especially religious experience, and which is not simply reducible to what we know of Jesus historically. Our faith-image of Jesus includes historical knowledge but it also includes myth and legend, our own ideals and hopes, the complex societal and parental influences that have given shape to our personal identities. At this point it may be helpful to analyze in greater detail first the nature of faith, then the nature of history, and finally to return to the question of their inter-relationship.

Faith, as already noted, is fundamentally interpersonal. As with all such human relationships, it involves trust, a basic willingness to step beyond the evidence in the strict sense of *proof* and to commit oneself to another person, with all the risk and vulnerability that such a step entails, even though all the evidence is not, nor ever can be, in. Without such willingness, human relationships are not possible. The ability to trust is what constitutes us as human persons in relationship. Thus, faith in this fundamental sense is universal in human experience. It is not peripheral to the human condition, an epiphenomenon, something superadded to human nature. Rather, some form of faith commitment is what constitutes us as human persons.

The prime analogy for Christian faith, then, is I-Thou relations. When we first meet someone, we go through a kind of historical-critical process of collecting information in order to get to know the person (name, background, interests, etc.), but if we are to move beyond a merely superficial interest to a truly human encounter, there comes a time in the relationship when we must entrust our deeper selves to the other. We will have reasonable grounds for making such a commitment on the basis of what we have learned and experienced of the person, but the true depth of all human relationships lies in this "leap of faith" beyond the evidence. A husband cannot *prove* in the strict sense that his wife loves him, but he *knows* it in the very process of mutual trust that forms the history of their relationship.

The word "process" implies that, once the initial commitment has been made, a kind of historical-critical knowledge continues to be operative in the relationship. Should the initial commitment prove to be false or misguided by what is learned subsequently, such knowledge can either destroy or at least radically alter the character of the relationship. It should be noted that it is in this sense that our Christian faith must always be open to, and will be seriously conditioned by, the results of biblical criticism. It is not that we should wait breathlessly for the latest results from scholars. Our faith commitment should be a firm one that does not vacillate with every new development, but it is also a living commitment with room for growth. In the process of our personal development, our faith-image of Jesus will grow and change. A study of biblical criticism will necessarily have a profound impact on that process.

The experience of trust is an experience of self-transcendence, a willingness to step beyond what can be strictly proved and to make a fundamental affirmation of the goodness of another person. As such it is a great risk, for in the very moment of entrusting ourselves we are at our most vulnerable. It is also a move beyond what is normally meant by historical knowledge. Yet, faith itself is an historical phenomenon, intrinsic to our historical consciousness, which is not simply reducible to historical-critical method. Faith properly belongs *within* the historical process as the appropriate and indispensable stance of human beings confronted with a world that has not yet arrived at its consummation. Without some form of faith commitment, being human at all is not possible. In this sense, faith is constitutive of the human precisely *as historical.*

On the other hand, faith is not reducible to history as that word is used by contemporary historians. History in this sense is a human science and/or art with very specific methodological rules. It is not a question of some abstract theory about the nature of history but rather of an analytical description of what historians actually do when they do history. Much of the confusion between historians and theologians arises from the use of the word "history" on different levels (e.g., Cullmann's "salvation-history"). There are certain things that an historian, *by reason of his method,* cannot call history, e.g., virginal conception, nature miracles, bodily resurrection. This is not to make a judgment one way or another about their actuality (unless one holds the philosophical stance that the *only* way of knowing anything is through the scientific or historical method), but simply to say that such judgments are beyond the limits of historical-critical methodology. This is perfectly legitimate. It is simply a recognition of the *limits* of the historical method. For example, an historian can deal both with the phenomenon that shortly after the death of Jesus certain of his disciples claimed that he was alive and with the effect of this claim upon subsequent history. These are historical phenomena that lie within the limiting

parameters of birth and death. But the historian, in terms
of historical method, cannot verify the truth or falsity of
the claim itself. Whether or not Jesus was actually raised
from the dead simply transcends the criteria of assent to
which the historian subscribes. Its verification lies in a different dimension, namely that of faith.

Historians, when they actually do history, subscribe to
what Van Harvey calls a certain morality of knowledge, an
ethic of assent. The "texture" or quality of assent is the
key element, i.e., not seeking to elicit a "heavier" kind of
assent than the evidence can bear. Harvey describes the
historian's craft as involving autonomy, assessment, and
sound judgment. Autonomy refers to the will to truth, the
conviction that one must think for oneself and not accept
sources as authoritative uncritically. The task of the historian is to confer authority on sources through critical
method. Assessment refers to the will to communication,
the recognition that history is a matter of public knowledge
(as distinct from belief or opinion) and so demands logical
candor and the giving of reasons to justify one's claims.
The best analogy is the law court: what sort of case does
one make to defend a certain claim? This leads into an
analysis of the structure of argument which on the level of
form is similar in all justificatory argumentation. One for-
mulates a question, considers the various likely candidates,
chooses a particular candidate based on the evidence, and
eliminates the alternatives. The evidence involves drawing
a conclusion from certain data based on warrants which
are usually implicit but which can offer further reasons for
moving from data to conclusion. This is not unlike the
syllogism of ancient logic except that there is no logical
necessity to the conclusion. It can be challenged on the
basis of other evidence and so require a qualification, or

else the warrant might require further backing. More interesting than the formal structure of argument, however, is the recognition that history is a field-encompassing field made up of a great diversity of arguments, data, and warrants. The historian appeals to such sciences as epigraphy and archaeology, seeks to reconstruct the original situation and to assess accurately the principal agents, and interprets the meaning of the events in a larger context. In all of this, the historian must have, finally, a sound sense of judgment. S/he must recognize that there are levels of judgment here that call for a differentiated quality of assent. The "texture" of that assent may range all the way from simple fact to very broad generalization. The degree of probability, and hence the appropriate qualifications, will shift accordingly.

The recognition of the complex nature of historical argument, its field-encompassing character, means that the historian's present standpoint in relation to the past must be conceived as a critically interpreted standpoint. It is not reducible simply to scientific knowledge, although science does help to distinguish the possible from the impossible. There are some things we simply cannot accept as real or factual, and so we correctly retain the right to disbelieve or to be skeptical about certain kinds of reports from the past. In fact, the scientific revolution has become so much a part of the furniture of our minds that we frequently take for granted knowledge that would have been unintelligible two thousand years ago, e.g., the use of electric lightbulbs as Bultmann was fond of pointing out.

On the other hand, it is important to recognize the uniqueness of every event. It is the task of the historian to enter imaginatively into the past and to understand the events in terms of their concrete context. This is the princi-

ple of correlation that affirms the time-space interconnec-
tedness of all historical events. Yet, it must be recognized,
especially as one moves from simple fact to the more complex questions of motives, purposes, or desires, that this is
an imaginative reconstruction in which one sets up certain
hypotheses about the situation and the principal agents.
Such hypotheses can only be confirmed on the basis of the
evidence, so that the final judgment may range from a high
degree of probability to a low degree of possibility. This is
the principle of criticism which recognizes that judgments
of probability are always open to revision. Finally, the
basic presupposition, however one justifies it philosophi-
cally, is one of common sense, namely that human beings
have enough in common that a contemporary historian can
truly enter into the situation of someone who lived two
thousand years ago. This is the principle of analogy which
affirms that our present experience cannot be radically dis-
similar to the experience of past persons if we are to make
any historical judgments at all.

The purpose of this brief review of Harvey's description
of history is simply to emphasize the fact that historians set
certain *methodological limits* in what they are willing to
affirm as historical. Every science, necessarily and legiti-
mately, sets limits for the purpose of method. The difficulty for faith arises when the stance is taken on philosophical grounds that the *only way* we know is historically. This
leads theologians either to expand the notion of history so
that it is correlative to the content of faith or to reduce the
content of faith to what we can know through historical
method. This frequently means, in the central and crucial
case for Christian faith of the resurrection of Jesus, that
one either seeks to establish the resurrection as an historical event or to reduce it to a mythological expression of a

faith experience, the latter being the only historical "event." What is being proposed here is a way out of this dilemma by differentiating faith and history as different ways of knowing that are distinct yet inseparably interrelated.

What then, to return to the initial statement of the problem, is the function of historical knowledge (in the technical sense just described) in relation to our faith knowledge of Jesus? Our proposed "solution" is that historical/historic knowledge has a *subordinate but indispensable* role to play in the formation of our "faith-image" of Jesus.

If our primary relationship to Jesus is one of faith, as Perrin affirms, then historical knowledge would appear to be *subordinate*. If history is a field-encompassing field that makes a great diversity of claims, faith likewise makes a great diversity of claims, among which are historical claims. Faith itself, as we have seen, properly belongs *within* history as the appropriate and necessary stance in a "not-yet" world, but at the same time it is a kind of knowledge that enables us to transcend the inevitable limitations of scientific historical knowledge. Faith makes claims that historians, by reason of their method, can neither affirm nor deny for they lie outside the limiting parameters of birth and death and they are based on God's revelatory activity. The primary claim, of course, is that in Jesus' resurrection is revealed the end of history, God's intention for the whole of created reality. This, by definition, is beyond history.

But, then, does our faith knowledge need historical knowledge at all? Given that Christian faith is deeply rooted in human history and human experience, it would seem to be *indispensable*. Without it, as the new questers

have noted, our faith would lose its rootedness in the personal history of Jesus and we would be in danger of committing ourselves to a mythological Lord. Perrin sees a
positive, a negative, and a direct function that historical
knowledge plays in relation to faith knowledge. While
what we know of Jesus historically can be a *direct* and
powerful source for preaching in the contemporary world
(insofar as we can stand in a relationship to the teaching
and person of Jesus similar to the memory impression of
the early church) and while, as well, such knowledge
concretizes our faith-image of Jesus in a *positive* sense
(what would our image of Jesus be like if we had only the
letters of Paul and not the four Gospels?), still the most
important of these functions is the *negative* control that
such knowledge exercises over false or inappropriate faith-
images of Jesus. Historical knowledge prevents us from
creating Jesus in our own image. It allows Jesus to be
Jesus, to stand over against us and challenge our presuppositions and, indeed, our prejudices. To those who would
claim Jesus, whether for a "right-wing" ideology that
seeks to justify the *status quo* of systemic oppression or for
a "left-wing" ideology that seeks to justify violent revolution, the best and indeed only answer is an appeal to
what we know of Jesus historically. Such knowledge does
not exhaust all we can say of Jesus in faith but it does serve
to control excesses and misdirections and to allow Jesus in
his own historical uniqueness to stand as challenge and
call.

Faith indeed is a risk, not by setting us in opposition to
the human and historical, but by drawing us ever more
deeply into the human and historical. Jesus "as he really
was" cannot simply be identified with the Jesus reconstructed through critical-historical methods but neither can

he be separated from such historical knowledge. Historical study cannot confirm or prove the affirmations of our faith, thus giving us a kind of certainty that will remove all doubt. Neither can historical study simply be relegated to an incidental and unimportant factor in a faith that claims its own self-authenticating ground, thus removing itself from any real involvement in the vagaries and ambiguities of human history and human experience. Both approaches seek a kind of certitude that faith cannot provide, a safe haven that will deliver us from life's insecurities and doubts. The position proposed here does recognize that faith gives us certainty, but it is the self-involving kind of certainty that allows us to *trust* in a promised future. As Leander Keck points out, the importance of historical knowledge is to know in whom we trust and what he stood for. Mere assertion is not enough.

Faith is interpersonal, a willing response to a loving Word. If Jesus is God's Word, then encounter with him, whether mediated historically or mythically or mystically, is indispensable to the nature of Christian faith. Historical knowledge is a subordinate but necessary medium to image forth this Jesus to whom we respond in faith. Jesus himself, in his personal identity, is and always has been decisive for Christian faith. The fact that only Jesus, of all the men and women down through the ages, has evoked such a relationship of faith in its religious sense points to his uniqueness.

Yet, knowledge of the historical Jesus, that Jesus who calls us forth in a concrete, self-involving way to take up our cross and actually follow him in specific *praxis,* working to realize the promised future of God's Kingdom, has been one of the major guiding motifs of that movement in theology which has come to be known as liberation theology. It is here that we see interest in the historical Jesus come to a culminating focus in contemporary theology, especially but not exclusively within Catholic sensibilities.

2) *Following the historical Jesus to liberation: a practical "application"*

Jon Sobrino suggests that there have been two phases of the Enlightenment: the first, embodied in Immanuel Kant, has sought the liberation of reason from all authoritarianism; and the second, embodied in Karl Marx, has sought the liberation of human beings from the actual wretched conditions in which they find themselves. So far, we have treated the question of the historical Jesus primarily in terms of the first Enlightenment and appropriately so, for the history of the question has been couched in these terms. The concern has been to address the crisis of meaning in theoretical terms, i.e., to find a rational solution to the problem of the relation between history and faith. The approach has been to think about the problem and to draw upon the resources of philosophical and historical thinking in order to resolve any apparent contradictions. The goal has been to come up with a coherent theory that will adequately resolve all the antinomies into an integrated and unified whole, to satisfy the mind's inherent desire for rationality.

Liberation theology, on the other hand, follows Marx in maintaining that it is more important to *change* reality than to understand it. The crisis is not so much one of meaning (in an abstract and theoretical sense) as of the concretely experienced conditions of reality itself. Contemporary experience is the primary resource for theological reflection, not the experience of the privileged bourgeois who are contributing to the oppression of the poor but the experience of the "other," the "nonperson," the oppressed who are the truly poor. According to Gustavo Gutiérrez, the exploited sectors of society, the despised races, the marginalized cultures are the historical subject of a new understanding of the faith. (See my "Jesus From the Other Side of History," pp. 258–261.) Theology must reflect upon *this* reality, which is only possible if those doing the reflecting actually enter into and participate in the lived experience of the poor and oppressed in their struggle for liberation. This too creates a crisis of meaning, as Roger Haight points out, in the concrete actuality of the enormity of human suffering on our planet, both in its extent and in the degree of its destructiveness for human potential (see *An Alternative Vision,* p. 34). No one with moral sensitivity can be indifferent to this overwhelming experience of human suffering.

With this in mind, the tools of analysis in liberation theology will be less those of philosophy (though it still has a valuable role to play) and more those of contemporary social sciences (especially those that explore the cultural, economic, and political factors that have given shape to society as it is). Moreover, if the starting point is not so much the deposit of truths that have been handed down in the tradition but the concrete and particular experiential practice of people here and now, then *orthopraxis* (actual involvement in particular and specific commitments) becomes much more important than *orthodoxy* (correct thinking and doctrine which tends to be general and abstract). For Sobrino, this means that *the* method of theological understanding is discipleship, i.e., the actual taking up of one's cross and following Jesus on the way. All other methods (history, social sciences, hermeneutics, systematics, criticism) are necessary but subordinate to the primacy of following Jesus.

The primary access to this Jesus, however, is not historical criticism but contemporary experience, the experience of the poor and oppressed who "speak Christ" today. This experience allows us to read the New Testament with new eyes. In technical terms, it combines a "hermeneutics of suspicion" with a "hermeneutics of hope." A hermeneutics of suspicion will not allow us to accept contemporary (or traditional) interpretations of reality, much less of the Bible, at face value. The suspicion is that such interpretations mask an ideology, i.e., a justification of the *status quo* while simultaneously hiding or ignoring the realities of oppression based in class, race, or sex. Ideologies, in a word, refuse to admit that we need to *change* reality. A hermeneutics of hope affirms precisely that we can change reality by way of personal involvement in the struggle for liberation through very specific options for action. Jesus' proclamation of the Kingdom of God correlates with such a hermeneutic. Although the initiative and final realization of the Kingdom is in the hands of the transcendent God, this God of Jesus works through the mediation of human response and responsibility (see my summary of Jesus' preaching in the introduction). Liberation, the salvific process of building the Kingdom of God, is occurring already within the processes of historical reality, even though its final consummation, the liberation of the whole of creation, lies beyond history within the mystery of God's intention and power.

Indispensable to the method of discipleship is the ability to perceive the way in which Jesus actually lived his life. Jesus is the one who was present, actively involved, in the struggle of the poor and oppressed. Not the "Word become flesh," which has given rise to much philosophical speculation in the history of theology, but the "God become poor," the God who in Jesus' lifestyle manifests a clear preferential option for the poor, is the decisive thing. Jesus' free human response to the Father's initiative in sending him on mission, his faithfulness to that mission even in the midst of the persecution and rejection that led to the cross, has revealed and made available for all of humankind the possibility of exercising human freedom in the building up of the Kingdom of God. Jesus' life and death is an invitation to participate in what he stood for: the liberation of self, society, and nature through complete and total dedication to the will of God. That will is manifest in the way Jesus walked with the poor and oppressed, with slaves, women, and children, those most marginated in a male-dominated society. It is only when we follow Jesus in our own societal context of oppression and actually stand under the cross with Jesus that we will finally "under-stand" who Jesus is (Christology) and, inseparably, who we are as disciples (ecclesiology).

If there is anything really new and unique about Latin American liberation theology, it lies in the claim that the poor and the oppressed can and should speak Christ in ways that up to this point in history have not been heard, that they are "the historical subject of a new understanding of the faith" (Gutiérrez). What is immediate and irreplaceable is the *praxis* of the people. This praxis includes both memory, the recognition of themselves in their history, culture, spirituality, and communal experience, and imagination, the critical appropriation of that memory in creatively new ways (through concrete and specific options) that will build the Kingdom by creating a new humanity (see my "Jesus From the Other Side of His-

tory," pp. 277 ff). Inseparable from and indispensable to
this claim is the impact of Jesus upon historical consciousness. This Jesus is commonly designated in the writings of
the liberation theologians as the "historical Jesus," but
such a designation raises two interconnected problems.
The first concerns the use of the historical-critical method
and the second the extent to which this historical Jesus is
normative for Christian faith.

Jon Sobrino's *Christology at the Crossroads* is illustrative of the first problem. What follows is elaborated in
greater detail in my article cited above (pp. 271–275). The
basic weakness that I see in Sobrino's approach is that he
wants to claim too much about the historical Jesus without
sufficient evidence. For example, how do we know that
Jesus remained faithful to the Father in unconditional
trust and absolute obedience? We can know historically
that Jesus in word and deed proclaimed a loving and caring
Father and called for such a response of trust, but Bultmann's famous objection about the possibility that Jesus
himself broke down and went to the cross railing against
his fate cannot be glossed over historically. Sobrino's
chapter on the faith of Jesus is illustrative of the problem.
He wishes to maintain two stages in the life of Jesus: the
springtime in Galilee and the crisis in Galilee that led to
Jerusalem, the latter involving a real shift for Jesus himself
in terms of his understanding of his mission. But can this
be established on historical grounds? Sobrino's desire to
concentrate on the history of Jesus' faith as it unfolded for
him personally is impossible without a chronological biography of Jesus, precisely what exegetes have denied since
the work of Karl Ludwig Schmidt on the framework of
Mark's Gospel.

Sobrino's approach, methodologically, is closer to the Gospel of Mark than to the historical Jesus. What he means by historical is kerygmatic. He refers to the liberation of the Hebrews as "a historical statement about God" insofar as "the whole historical process of liberation is attributed to God's intervention" (p. 322). But as soon as the idea of God's intervention is introduced, one moves from strictly historical to kerygmatic statements, i.e., the proclamation of God's saving acts in history. The Gospel of Mark is clearly written in the light of such a divine intervention, the resurrection of Jesus. It identifies the Christ of faith with the Jesus of history. So, apparently, does Sobrino, but then it would be better to drop the adjective "historical" when speaking about Jesus in this manner. We know that Jesus remained faithful to the Father because the Father raised him from the dead and so vindicated him. This is a theological, not an historical, statement, insofar as it is talking about the action of God as vindication of Jesus.

It is only in the light of the total Christ as risen that we can affirm with theological certitude that Jesus lived to the end a life of unconditional trust and absolute obedience to the Father's will. Sobrino's Christology, it seems to me, is fundamentally a retelling of Jesus' story with close similarities to the Gospel of Mark. Both Mark and Sobrino employ historical materials, but by not distinguishing clearly between the historical Jesus and the Christ of faith, both are able to say much more about Jesus than strictly historical judgment will allow. The point here is that, in the light of the contemporary discussion concerning the quest of the historical Jesus, one cannot use the adjective "historical" indiscriminately. This is not to deny the powerful relevance

of what both Mark and Sobrino have to say about Jesus
for the contemporary situation.

This leads to the second problem: the extent to which the
historical Jesus is normative for Christian faith. Is he *the*
norm, or one among several? Roger Haight argues for the
latter:

> Christology . . . inevitably requires a holding together in
> balance, in mutual and self-critical tension, a variety of
> norms: the historical Jesus who is being interpreted, the
> original, originating, and constituting interpretations of
> Jesus that are found in the New Testament, interpretations
> of Jesus from Christian history and tradition, and our own
> historical situation which provides the context and lan-
> guage for our own interpretations of Jesus and the partic-
> ular focus for it. (*Alternative,* p. 318, n. 3.)

In all of this, Jesus remains normative for Christian
faith, but it is the human Jesus as variously interpreted
through the generations and not simply reducible to what
we can say of him in strictly historical terms. The tension
between past and present experience is extremely important for the question of normativity. The power of Sobrino's Christology is that he retells the story of Jesus in
the light of the contemporary experience of oppression. A
simple repetition of the past (the *memoria Jesu*) is not
enough, for Jesus continues to live today in new and unforeseen ways through the eyes of the poor who are able to
imagine new possibilities. Thus, a creative tension will
always exist between memory and imagination, between
past tradition and contemporary experience. While liberation theology employs all the norms mentioned above,
surely the most crucial is the contemporary experience of
following Jesus in the struggles of the poor. For Sobrino,

the method of discipleship is the most radical and thorough verification of whatever we might say about Jesus, especially that he is the eternal Son of the Father.

In sum, liberation theology involves an "epistemological break" that focuses not so much on progressive development and fulfillment (analogical thinking) as on contradiction and transformation (dialectical thinking). The motive for doing theology is not so much to contemplate the wonders of creation as to eliminate its contradictions, the suffering caused by human sinfulness. Thus, the question of God and evil (theodicy) is not resolved by a new and better conceptualization but by overcoming the power of sin in the actual transformation of the world. The cross of Jesus represents the God who suffers in order to transform the world from within actual historical processes. In all of this, it is crucially important to emphasize that the primary focus is the following of Jesus, not Marxist class analysis. If Marx is used at all, it is as one of several ancillary methods that can help to clarify the situation of the contemporary world.

The recent *Instruction* (August 6, 1984) of the Vatican Congregation for the Doctrine of the Faith, entitled "Certain Aspects of the Theology of Liberation" (Roger Haight in *Alternative* appends the whole text and offers an interpretation of it, pp. 257–291), expresses its purpose as follows: ". . . to draw the attention of pastors, theologians, and all the faithful to the deviations and risks of deviation, damaging to the faith and to Christian living, that are brought about by certain forms of liberation theology which use, in an insufficiently critical manner, concepts borrowed from various currents of Marxist thought." While this caution is valid and legitimate, it is difficult to know if it was directed at any particular liberation theologian. Moreover, as Haight's analysis shows, the document proposes a hypothetical construct of a holistic system that does not seem to be present in the work of any theologian. Thus, the document seems to be aimed only at anyone who is committed to a holistic view of Marxism, not to anyone who simply uses elements of Marx's thought in an ancillary way. An historical analogy is the condemnation of Aristotle as a holistic system in the thirteenth century, yet Thomas Aquinas' use of elements in Aristotle's system was key to the development of scholastic philosophy.

The *Instruction* speaks of the truth about Jesus, the church, and human dignity as the "indispensable pillars of liberation." I know of no major theologian who would disagree. The concern for conflict in society, as well as in the church, does not derive from any particular philosophical system, least of all from Marxist economic determinism, but from the actual experience of oppression and violence in the contemporary world. And the inspiration for an appropriately Christian response to such systemic evil is found not in Marx but in Jesus. As Haight notes, the document itself "is very sympathetic to the perceptions and values that underlie liberation theology" (p. 258). In fact, the first half of the document is a strong endorsement of the preferential option for the poor and of all those who are engaged in the struggle for true liberation. Thus, this *Instruction,* however valid and legitimate the concerns it actually expresses, should not be used as a political tool against the legitimate concerns of liberation theology.

It should be noted in conclusion that liberation theology is not confined to Latin America. It is especially powerful and relevant in situations of oppression in Asia and Africa as well as in Latin America, but it also offers "an alternative vision" to much wider socio-cultural and theological environments, as Roger Haight demonstrates. A favorite text of all liberation theologians is Paul's invocation of an early baptismal formula: "For as many of you as were baptized into Christ have put on Christ. There is neither Jew nor Greek, there is neither slave nor free, there is neither male nor female; for you are all one in Christ Jesus" (Gal. 3:27-28). The Christian experience, begun in baptism, must always be one of liberation from racism, classism, and sexism. Paul's threefold reference to these socio-cultural relationships has, each in turn, received greater or lesser attention and focus in different epochs. Each has its roots in the historical ministry of Jesus, and each continues in new forms in contemporary times.

Thus, the main focus and emphasis in early Christianity, especially among the Pauline communities, was on the relationship between Jew and Greek. "But now in Christ Jesus you who once were far off have been brought near in the blood of Christ. For he is our peace, who has made us both one, and has broken down the dividing wall of hostility . . ." (Eph. 2:13-14). Paul's mission to the Gentiles was rooted in Jesus' challenge to the ethnocentrism of his contemporaries. The Kingdom of God is for all, and especially for those considered to be outsiders: the poor, the oppressed, the marginated, and the Gentiles. The sad fact of history, however, is that Gentile inclusion eventually led to the rejection of our common Jewish heritage and the erection of new walls of hostility. In our own times and country, the need to overcome racism is expressed in James Cone's black theology, in Vine Deloria's God who is red, and in Virgilio Elizondo's Mexican-American promise, among others. All of these movements are rooted in the contemporary experience of racism and appeal to the historical Jesus as one who provides a searing critique of our racist culture.

The relationship between slave and free, as a Christian imperative to eradicate all forms of slavery, came into focus much later, and not clearly until the Enlightenment and its subsequent social movements. But this too had its roots in Jesus' challenge to master-slave forms of domination. "You know that those who are supposed to rule over the Gentiles lord it over them, and their great men exercise authority over them. But it shall not be so among you; but whoever would be great among you must be your servant, and whoever would be first among you must be slave of all" (Mark 10:42–44). Those who would follow Jesus must learn to serve, not to dominate. Yet, sadly, how much evil has been committed in the name of a false image of Jesus Christ as imperial Lord. The Latin American theologians know well that the abolition of slavery as an institution has not meant the end of oppression and enslavement. The colonization of the Americas by European conquerors in the sixteenth century has been replaced by another form of colonization, economic exploitation that continues to keep vast masses of people in servitude and virtual slavery. This is the contemporary form of classism (and racism). It is against this that liberation theologians in Latin America, Asia, and Africa have issued a call for liberation in the name of Jesus who once identified himself with the poor and the oppressed and still does so today.

Finally, the relationship between male and female is just now emerging into greater focus, and it is indeed the most important liberation movement of all. For, at least in the conviction of this writer, every liberation movement will be truncated, i.e., will fail to achieve full human liberation, unless and until it includes the liberation of the image of God as male and female (Gen. 1:27). All forms of oppression based on race, class, or sex are interconnected, but the male-female relationship lies at the heart of all human relationships. If this relationship does not manifestly express full freedom and equality, then the intention of God in creating human beings is frustrated. This is rooted, once again, in Jesus' ministry among, for, and with women. In the context of his times, Jesus' attitude toward and treatment of women was remarkable. He had female disciples who openly accompanied him as he traveled about in his public ministry. He included Mary in the circle of his male disciples in direct contradiction to the traditional role of women as represented by Martha (Luke 10:38–42). He spoke publicly with women who were strangers, healed them, praised their faith, pointed to them as examples of how God acts. Examples could be multiplied, but the important point is that he broke through the oppression of women and, in so doing, offered a new vision of humanity. Elisabeth Schüssler-Fiorenza puts it succinctly: "The woman-identified man, Jesus, called forth a discipleship of equals that still needs to be discovered and realized by women and men today" (*In Memory of Her,* p. 154). Again, the sad fact of history is that Christianity developed within a social context that was androcentric and patriarchal. Accommodation to Jewish and Greco-Roman patriarchy, already in the New Testament itself, led to the suppression of women's experience. Liberation theologians who are feminist seek to reclaim women's experience as the focus of contemporary theologizing. Among Christian feminists, this is not an attempt to turn the tables and replace patriarchy with matriarchy. All liberation theologians recognize that true freedom can never be achieved if the oppressed simply become the oppressors. The goal is a new humanity, which is only possible if the full human potential of women is included. In this, feminist theologians, as all liberation theologians, find an ally in the historical Jesus whose vision, and *praxis,* of true liberation offers a radical and challenging critique of the oppressor-oppressed dialectic throughout human history and, above all, in our own times.

Thus, in this brief review of the varieties of liberation movements, the two points emphasized in Latin American liberation theology continue to be operative. The first is the primacy of contemporary experience, especially the experience of oppression in terms of race, class, and sex. The second is the indispensable importance of the historical Jesus as one who stands over against all such oppression and calls for the liberation of creation as a whole. Yet, emphasis upon this correlation between contemporary experience and the historical Jesus is not intended to ignore or deny the intervening two thousand years of Christian tradition. In all of this discussion, as we have seen, the question of normativity as involving a complex transmission of tradition from past to present emerges over and over. With this in mind, the final section will attempt to integrate the contemporary discussion into a more synthetic view.

3) *Jesus as the "root-metaphor" of Christian faith*

It is truly imagination that saves us. How can faith survive in the face of history, i.e., of the "underside" of history, of that which confronts us with so many contradictions to our most cherished beliefs? Two Greek words catch the contrast and interplay of our contemporary dilemma. *Poiēsis* (artistic creativity) engages the imagination even when, and especially when, *praxis* (any concrete and specific action) fails. *Poiēsis* recognizes the priority of the Spirit and the provisionality of our *praxis*. *Praxis*, if separated from *poiēsis*, tends to be overly serious and moralistic and can easily degenerate into a kind of "works righteousness." *Poiēsis* recognizes that the God of history is also the God of creation, that the good news is life, recreative and full of unexpected possibility, even in the face of its contradiction. The cross, as symbolizing the failure of human freedom, almost demands resurrection, the affirmation of a God whose creativity will "finish the work" of creation, bring it to its fulfillment. Yet, the symbol of resurrection does not negate human freedom. Much rather, it *enables* human freedom to go into action (*praxis*) in many ways previously unforeseen and unimagined. Resurrection means that we believe in a God who has the imaginative audacity to dance on his own grave, a God who creatively validates that the kind of life Jesus lived in self-sacrificing love does indeed have a future, right here and now, in our own lives. To do the truth (*praxis*) is, in the final analysis, to create the beautiful (*poiēsis*), to rejoice in the freedom of the Spirit.

What is coming to the forefront of contemporary biblical criticism and what can, I think, afford a more synthetic view of the diversities of approach within biblical scholarship is the *primacy of story*. In the light of our preceding discussion, one can see four reasons for this: a reassessment of the Enlightenment, a new understanding of literary criticism, a renewed appreciation of the narrative base for all liberation, and a deeper realization of the narrative quality of human experience as such.

First, the Enlightenment, while seeking to deny any value to myth, has given rise to its own myth, the myth of modernity which, as Terrence Tilley points out, "is *the story that kills stories* . . . The myth of the enlightenment is a story that tells us we have outgrown stories. It tells us that narratives are irrelevant to truth and truth is irrelevant to narratives" (*Story Theology,* p. 35). In the world of pure reason, thinkers celebrate the autonomy and independence of ourselves and our world, the progress of the world through evolutionary change, and the complete separation of science, which gives us clear, objective fact (what is "true"), from art, which appeals to subjective feelings through the use of the imagination. The irony is that "modernity" has simply substituted one set of myths for another. We just tell a different story, but one that needs to be balanced by the recognition that there is not one, but a multiplicity of stories.

Second, the history of the scholarly quest for the historical Jesus, as outlined in chapter two, is basically a quest for method. Source criticism led to form criticism. Form criticism has led, in turn, to a new appreciation of how the final editors of the Gospels have both employed sources and transformed them in their final composition (redaction criticism). Related methods have focused upon the audience for which the work was written and the social setting out of which it came, as well as the history of its transmission and interpretation. All of this has led to a new appreciation of *the work itself.* This generally comes under the rubric of literary criticism. The previous methods (source, form, redaction, etc.) put stress on an historical analysis of the *genesis* of a text. Literary criticism stresses the interpretation of the text *as literature.* This is in contrast to an earlier understanding of literary criticism, usually found in New Testament introductions, which discuss such "background" issues as authorship, date, sources, stages of composition, etc. William Beardslee summarizes the new view well:

> . . . the approach of literary criticism is to accept the form of the work, and the reader's participation in the form, as an intrinsic part of entry into the imaginative world of the work. Hence literary criticism is not as eager as many modern theological interpreters are to move out of the world of myth; its primary quest is for what the imaginative world of the work in question is (*Literary Criticism,* p. 13).

This implies a different understanding of what the Bible is. As Tilley notes: "The fact that the Bible *contains* stories was supplanted by the recognition that the Bible is *composed of* stories—myths, legends, satires, allegories, histories, apocalyptic, parable, etc. This marks a significant shift in vision" (*Story Theology,* p. 29). The Bible is primarily narrative in character, and everything in it must be understood in the context of *story.* At the same time, the Bible is a veritable *library* of diverse literary types or genres. Literary criticism embraces this rich diversity and the pluralism it implies. It eschews any view that would reduce the Bible to a single form or conceptualization in favor of an inclusive understanding of "a variety of visions" (Beardslee).

Amos Wilder, in his analysis of the earliest modes and genres of "Christian rhetoric," notes the following characteristics: brevity, creative novelty, dramatic immediacy (dialogic), use of the common language of the day (koine Greek), emphasis upon communal experience (popular or folkloric?), and most importantly for our thesis addiction to narrative as "the basic speech-mode of Christianity" (*Early Christian Rhetoric,* pp. 18–35). One can classify the

genres into larger wholes (e.g., gospel, acts, letter, apoca-
lypse) or into smaller units (e.g., parables, proverbs,
poems), but such classifications should not simply be identified with or confined to Western aesthetic norms. The
New Testament does not fit neatly into either Greco-
Roman models or later literary classics. The uniqueness of
the Gospel as "a new outburst and plenitude of human
utterance and communication in all aspects of language"
(Wilder, *Rhetoric,* p. 128) must be preserved. Yet, para-
doxically, while the world of the New Testament remains
strange and remote, the language has become almost too
familiar, the story routinized, the myths devalued. As
Beardslee suggests, the failure to communicate may not be
so much one of loyalty (faith) as of "imaginative participation" (*Literary Criticism,* pp. 10–11). This is the key to
understanding the primacy of story over other methods
that are also designed to understand and interpret the
Bible.

The third reason for moving story to the forefront is the
emphasis in liberation theology on the concrete experience
and *praxis* of the people. All true liberation is based in
memory and imagination. The "subversive memory" of a
people or group that has been oppressed is to tell their own
story, a story that has been suppressed and denied by the
oppressing powers. This, in many ways, is the most important thing that the oppressed can and should do. Yet, the
purpose is not simply to recover a past that is gone forever
but to move toward *praxis* that is true *poiēsis,* i.e., to tell
the story by living it in new and creative ways. Basically,
liberation theologians are retelling the Christian story in
the light of contemporary experience. Jesus lives *now* in
the face of an oppressed Indian, and it is the same Jesus
who lived *then.* His story continues to be told wherever

and whenever the poor and rejected are crucified. Thus, liberation theology has a narrative basis of necessity. What is said of liberation applies to all human experience. This brings us to our fourth reason.

The narrative quality of all human experience is grounded in the processive and durational character of historical experience (history = our story) in which the future is experienced as coming through the past into the present. The present "moment," if isolated from the ongoing movement of experience for the sake of analysis, is an abstraction from the "inherently durational" character of human experience. If our experience is, in fact, basically durational, then the best way to talk about it is to tell stories. This does not deny the need for critical analysis (historical, philosophical, psychosocial), but such analyses always remain subordinate to the primacy of the story, however indispensable. "The implication of this view is that without a story that is both faithful to our ongoing experiences and actions, and examined critically for its truthfulness, we cannot be fully human" (Tilley, *Story Theology,* p. 26; see pp. 23–26 for his use of the work of Stephen Crites). Full humanity, the liberation of creation, was the concern of Jesus in his prophetic ministry. He communicated what he wanted to say about the Kingdom of God primarily by telling stories. The concentration on the parables of Jesus (the interpretation of which in the past twenty years has been one of the major contributions of American scholarship) is one of the most assured and fruitful results of the quest for the historical Jesus.

The question that this raises, at its root, is how God communicates with us, i.e., how revelation occurs. God's self-communication is always mediated through language, the Word, for human beings are best described as symbol-

making animals, not in spite of but precisely because of
their embodied nature and historical rootedness. Given the
complexities of human linguistic activity, a further question arises as to what is primary and what is secondary.
The thesis presented here is that language on the level of
symbol-metaphor-story is primary, and that language on
the level of description and/or definition is secondary,
subordinate (however indispensable) to the primacy of
symbol.

Symbolic experience that comes to metaphorical expression is the primordial way of being human because it
touches upon and seeks to give expression to that which is
rooted in the deepest mysteries of life, including our relationship to God, to self, to others in society, to our bodies,
and to the whole of nature. Following the analysis of Paul
Ricoeur (as interpreted by Sallie McFague, *Metaphorical
Theology,* pp. 119–122), we live within symbol as the pre-
linguistic bonding of ourselves to the cosmos. Yet, to be
human, symbolic experience necessarily comes to expression (the level of articulation) as metaphor. Thus, as
Ricoeur himself puts it, symbolic infrastructure and metaphorical superstructure are intertwined. We never have
"raw experience" (any more than complete intelligibility),
but experience that is always mediated through linguistic
interpretation. As McFague puts it: "Symbols need metaphors, for without them they lose their rootedness in life.
Metaphor articulates symbolic richness, making distinctions, suggesting alternative interpretations, insisting on
the tension in which we always exist in relation to reality"
(p. 120). Metaphor is the most fundamental and primary
level of articulation because it retains the tensive wholeness
of the symbolic experience. Yet it also leads to conceptualization. Metaphors need conceptual clarity and preci-

sion, just as concepts need the multivalent complexity of metaphor.

Metaphor constitutes us in our humanness at a most basic level. It is the simple ability to *associate* one thing with another, to *see* the unfamiliar through the familiar, to *discover* new relationships and possibilities. It is the way every child learns. A metaphor quite simply says: A = B. It is not merely a rhetorical device, ornamental but replaceable by some other type of speech. Nor is it a simile (A is *like* B) which tends to soften the sense of identity and tension. Rather, it places two active thoughts in a tensive interaction, such that the understanding of each term is affected by the other. The instinctive reaction to metaphors is to say both yes and no, to affirm and deny the identity. McFague employs an example from Max Black: "War is a chess game." If the metaphor is living, it will tease the mind into active thought, seeing new possibilities in the tensive interaction of the two thoughts. The association of war and chess provides new insights into each, while at the same time blocking out other aspects. On the other hand, if the metaphor is dead, it will have become literalized or so commonplace as to go unnoticed (e.g., the arm of the chair). Finally, metaphor requires participation in its referent. One must actively enter into and live the experience of the game of chess at least to some degree— the deeper the personal involvement the better—in order to understand how it illumines war. A game is a kind of story. Tilley quite rightly points out (*Story Theology,* pp. 3ff) that in the final analysis one cannot understand a metaphor unless one knows the story (or game) that gives the metaphor its context. This is based again in the narrative quality of all human experience.

Parables, as noted in the introduction, are narrated

metaphors. When Jesus says the Kingdom of God *is* a
sower who went out to sow (Mark 4:3–9 par.), he is invit-
ing his listeners to enter into *this* experience in order to
enter into the Kingdom of God. And this experience is the
parabolic world created by Jesus. This particular story is
not all there is to the Kingdom of God, but to experience
this story is to experience the Kingdom of God. Jesus'
stories are remarkable in that he talks about the ordinary,
everyday experiences of his contemporaries. He invites
them to enter ever more deeply into their life experiences,
and yet precisely at the point of greatest familiarity he
reveals a new and unfamiliar way of seeing those same realities: an extravagant, superabundant harvest, a "good"
Samaritan, a "prodigal" father. He provides a "shock" to
the imagination and leaves the application open, for each
one must hear and respond in his or her own way. Thus,
the stories interpret the meaning of the various metaphors
Jesus employs to illumine his primary symbol, or root
metaphor, the Kingdom of God. (A root metaphor is a
dominant metaphor that is constitutive of a religious sensibility in such ways that to change the root metaphor would
involve a radical shift in religious understanding.) All of
these narrated metaphors, in a great variety of images,
truly express the reality of the Kingdom, yet no one of
them ever exhausts the possibilities of the mystery. Such
language can only evoke the mystery; it cannot describe or
define it.

Similarly, many authors (e.g., Keck, Donahue, Crossan,
McFague) speak of Jesus in the New Testament as the
parable of God. Mark's Gospel can be understood as parabolic in form. The New Testament uses a great variety of
imagery (metaphors) to bring to expression the mystery
that is Jesus. "Son of God" is certainly one of the central

metaphors. Yet, it is not this title, or any of the titles, that interprets the meaning of Jesus. On the contrary, it is in actually telling the story of Jesus in all its concreteness and particularity that Mark gives his main titles, "Christ," "Son of God," and "Son of Man," their meaning. Thus, the definitive confession of faith can only take place at the end of the story when the centurion, *seeing how he died,* said, "Truly this man was the Son of God" (Mark 15:39). It is the story of Jesus' way to the cross that tells us what the title "Son of God" really means.

In sum, symbol-metaphor-story, while distinct, form an inseparable unit. Every symbolic experience must come to metaphorical expression if it is to emerge in human consciousness in an accessible way. If one metaphor becomes dominant within the communal consciousness, it will inevitably seek further metaphorical expression in a rich variety of imagery, no one of which can express in a definitive and exhaustive way the depth of the originating symbolic experience. The metaphors in turn must inevitably come to narrative expression if they are to make sense, for it is only in story that they take on their full contextual meaning as human experience. I propose that in Scripture each epoch (Israel/Jesus/Church) has a root metaphor that has come to further metaphorical expression in narrative. Hence, the following schema:

PRIMARY LANGUAGE

	SYMBOL (root metaphor)		METAPHOR (rich variety)		STORY (context/meaning)
Israel:	YAHWEH	*is*	God of your Fathers	*who*	saves people
Jesus:	KINGDOM	*is*	a prodigal father	*who*	embraces son
Church:	JESUS	*is*	the beloved Son	*who*	dies with cry

Thus, in the post-resurrection church, Jesus is the root metaphor of Christian faith. The example is Mark's image of Jesus, but the point is again that Jesus comes to expression in a rich variety of images and stories, all of which tell us who he is and none of which exhausts his mystery.

The above schema raises two further issues. On the level of primary language, are there not several different types of stories, or are they all reducible to the parable as the primary form? Secondly, on the level of secondary language, does such language, once it emerges, displace the primary language by explaining what it all means in clear and precise terms, whether by definitions or by descriptions? In other words, what is the precise relationship between primary and secondary language?

In his chapter entitled "The Shapes of Stories," Terrence Tilley offers an illuminating distinction between myths, parables, and actions as at least three "shapes" that religious stories can take. "*Myths* are stories that set up worlds. Their polar opposites are *parables,* stories that upset worlds. Between these are *actions,* realistic stories set within worlds" (*Story Theology,* p. 39, following Crossan who also includes *apologues* that defend worlds and *satires* that attack worlds). Myths provide stability. They give us a sense of who we are and where we stand, i.e., a sense of identity in relation to the world. Their primary function is to reconcile contradictions, or at least to convince us that such mediation is permanently possible. "What myth does is not just to attempt the mediation in story of what is sensed as irreconcilable, but in, by, and through this attempt it establishes the possibility of reconciliation" (John Dominic Crossan, *The Dark Interval,* p. 53). Tilley refers to Joseph Campbell's analysis of the fourfold function of myth: *religious,* i.e., structuring our relation to transcendent mystery; *cosmological,* showing where the world came from and where it is going; *moral-social,* undergirding the social order; and *psychological,* providing individuals with their own space or role within society (pp. 42–44). Myths structure our world, and this is the only world we know. Interestingly, this fourfold function of myth is very similar to William Thompson's description of the "Jesus-event" (= Christology) as "the disclosure of a new vision and praxis of our relations to God, to self, to society, and to the world" (*The Jesus Debate,* p. vi & *passim*). The story of Jesus is fundamentally the myth that structures our world in this fourfold relationship.

Parables subvert the world created by myth. They challenge the assumptions of our myths and call us to change. "Parable is always a somewhat unnerving experience. You can usually recognize a parable because your immediate reaction will be self-contradictory: 'I don't know what you mean by that story but I'm certain I don't like it'." And further: "You have built a lovely home, myth assures us; but, whispers parable, you are right above an earthquake fault" (Crossan, pp. 56, 57). As Crossan emphasizes, parables are only possible in relation to myths. One can live in myth without parable, but parables live only in the tension created by subverting myth. Parable is not another myth, an "antimyth." Parables show the limits of our myths, their relativity. They shatter worlds. They generate new possibilities for those who have eyes to see and ears to hear.

We need both myth and parable, both harmony and tension, both the "Catholic sensibility" of continuity, order, and participation, and the "Protestant sensibility" of discontinuity, tension, and iconoclasm (see McFague, *Metaphorical Theology,* p. 13). We need to tell stories that structure our world and other stories that warn us against turning our constructions into idols and/or killing them through literalization. We also need stories that explore our world, halfway between myth and parable. These are actions. Most of our stories are of this type. Some are factual (history, biography, autobiography) and some are fictional (novels, short stories, allegories), but they all have this in common: they tell us how things go in a world (Tilley, *Story Theology,* p. 51). They give us the opportunity to explore, to rethink, to stretch the imagination. The story of Jesus takes all these shapes, and we must attend to them all if we would know who Jesus is and who we are as his disciples. Tilley summarizes: "A narrative theology of myth without parable would be stifling; of parable without myth would be baffling; of action alone would be boring" (p. 53).

As to the second issue, symbols that come to metaphorical expression in stories give rise to thought (Ricoeur). We need to move from this primary language to the secondary language of definitions and descriptions because the human mind asks questions and seeks answers that will satisfy the desire to know. Paul Ricoeur sees a threefold movement in the process of interpretation, which is understood to be a creative engagement or conversation between the text of a tradition and contemporary experience (see Thompson, *The Jesus Debate,* pp. 80–84). The first is an initial openness to what the text might say or the questions it might raise in the light of the interpreter's own experience. To relate it to Ricoeur's notion of symbol, we first experience symbol in a precritical and unreflective way. The second step is to engage in a critical process using the various methods available. We seek to move from the vagueness of a merely subjective sense of the symbol or text to a critical explanation of it. Here is where the *indispensable* character of biblical criticism comes into play: not only the historical-critical method, but also, as Thompson enumerates them, psychosocial-critical methods, philosophical-theological methods, and global analysis (other religions and cultures), as well as literary criticism insofar as it is a method supplying textual warrants. All of these methods involve the move to some form of conceptualization, either definitions that are abstract and propositional or descriptions that are experiential and historical. There is a natural progression from the more concrete to the more abstract because symbols demand interpretation. However, ontological language, as all language, remains symbolic. There is continuity, to be sure, but the danger is to think that our human conceptualizations and systems have "grasped" or exhausted the content of the mystery. Thus, the third step is the recognition of the *subordinate* character of all methods to the primacy of the symbol. Once we have gone through the process of critical appropriation and have been transformed by a new comprehension, we in fact return to the symbol and experience it ever anew with a second, postcritical naiveté. This process is a continuous spiral as the new experience of the symbol or text will give rise to new thought, etc.

In sum, Jesus is the primordial symbol or root metaphor of Christian faith. Neither subjective experience nor any "objective" system of thought can fully disclose him. Any such system, whether historical or philosophical, must recognize the *limits* of its own presuppositions and methods. The New Testament itself, as literary criticism shows, exhibits a great variety of stories about him, all of which attempt to bring to expression who he is. What all this means is that Jesus, in the mystery of his personal relationship to the divine reality, continually transcends any attempt that we make, whether in the New Testament or in the subsequent tradition of the church or in the present day, to bring to expression the mystery of his personhood. He remains the primordial symbol or root metaphor in the tensive, evocative sense of embodying more than can simply be articulated in abstract, propositional or historical, descriptive terms. Mystery can only be evoked. Symbol has power to evoke because it addresses itself to the whole person, to the imagination, the will, and the emotions, as well as to the intellect, and because it is deeply rooted in human experience and human history. Thus, it is "more adequate" to express mystery, although the mystery absolutely transcends the symbolic experience and expression of it as well. One cannot simply invent true symbols. They emerge from the depths of human consciousness, especially in the collective sense, and they will last as living symbols only as long as they continue to evoke those depths.

V. CONCLUSION

IS there a future for the historical Jesus? After considering the history of the quest, the attitude of the magisterium, and the concerns of contemporary biblical critics, it seems clear that knowledge of the historical Jesus will always be indispensable to Christian faith. On the other hand, this brief review of the question has also shown that such knowledge will always be subordinate to the faith both in its tradition and in its contemporary manifestations. Yet, the real issue is not just the importance of the historical Jesus but of the whole process of biblical criticism. In a word, there are simply no alternatives to biblical criticism if we wish to communicate the message of the Bible to today's world, both within and outside Christianity. It is finally a question of the nature of the Bible itself. As we have seen, a simple harmonization of the four Gospels destroys the distinctive and unique character of each Gospel. It assumes that we could write a fifth Gospel which somehow would be better than the four we have. Moreover, a naive fundamentalism that tends to reduce everything in the Bible to a literal one-to-one correspondence with a presumably available objective reality (the "facts") is equally destructive of the true nature of the Bible for it misses totally its literary character and the importance of story. Even a selective use of biblical texts in a liturgical setting can be harmful if the homilist does not know how to relate the individual selections to the artistic unity of the texts from which they are taken. An informed Catholic today cannot avoid the questions raised by biblical criticism if s/he wishes to be in touch with the foundational documents of the Christian faith. To tell the story we must

107

know it, both in its originating sources and in its impact
upon our own journeys.

All of this gives rise to the final question: what is the
authority of Scripture today? It lies, it seems to me, in our
ability to enter into the story through "imaginative participation." In the true sense of authority, no one can simply
tell us that the Bible is authoritative for us. To remain at
that level is to be arrested in one's own development and
growth at the level of the external, coercive kind of authority which a parent exercises when s/he perceives that a
child is intractable and nothing else will work. The Bible
becomes authoritative for us when we enter into the story
and find ourselves there. Jesus did not impose his vision
upon his listeners. He could not do that and still respect
their personal freedom and integrity. He invited his listeners to enter in—not just to peek in from a safe distance
but to resonate with the unfolding of the story so that they
could recognize its truth for themselves and say, "Yes, that
is the way things are; that says something about my life
that I had never realized before." The Gospel of Mark tells
us that we must take up our cross, in the concrete and specific conditions of our own lives, and follow Jesus "on the
way" (Mark 10:52). Only then will we truly know who
Jesus is and who we are as his disciples.

VI.   DISCUSSION QUESTIONS

1. What is your response to the image of Jesus portrayed in the introduction? Does it resonate with your own faith-image of him?

2. Why is the quest for the historical Jesus a "modern" question? Does this mean we have a superior viewpoint in relation to the past?

3. What was the principal result of the nineteenth-century quest? Why is it important for biblical criticism?

4. What further question did form criticism ask? What is the major difficulty that form criticism raises for the quest of the historical Jesus?

5. Why does R. Bultmann set up an opposition between history and faith? Do you prefer Barth's approach or Bultmann's? Why? Has the continuing concern for the original quest provided an adequate response to Bultmann?

6. What is the crucial issue of the new quest in opposition to Bultmann? How do you understand the significance of the "three divergences" from Bultmann in Bornkamm's *Jesus of Nazareth* (where he follows the earlier lead of Kaesemann and Fuchs)?

7. Why is Jesus' self-consciousness such an important issue in the new quest? How do you understand Jesus' consciousness? What is the source of your knowledge?

8. Why does James M. Robinson think that a new quest is both *possible* and *legitimate* today? Discuss the two problems that arise from his view.

9. Discuss Bultmann's famous response to the new quest. What is his view of kerygma? Why does this lead him to reject the new quest in principle?

10. Discuss the responses of Robinson and Ebeling to Bultmann. What is the fundamental problem? Which position do you prefer? Why?

11. Was the acceptance of biblical criticism important for Vatican II? Why? What is its significance for ecumenism? Is it important for other areas of church life?

12. Discuss the significance of *Divino Afflante Spiritu.* What key development does *Sancta Mater Ecclesia* endorse? Why is this important? What does it imply about the nature of Scripture? Why is *Dei Verbum* of such great importance in this discussion?

13. Do you subscribe to the proposition, "if it didn't happen, it isn't true"? Why or why not? How does this affect your understanding of Scripture?

14. What do you understand by history? By faith? How do you relate the two? Do you find yourself in greater sympathy with the position that tends to identify history and faith, that opposes them, or that seeks to mediate between the two? Explain.

15. What does it mean to say that historical knowledge has a subordinate but indispensable role to play in relation to faith? Do you agree with this position? Why?

16. What is the difference between the first and second phases of the Enlightenment? How does this difference affect the orientation of liberation theology? What, according to Sobrino, is *the* method of theological understanding? Explain.

17. What problems are raised by the appeal to the "historical Jesus" in liberation theology? What does this say about the methodological importance of contemporary experience in relation to the historical Jesus? Discuss this in relation to racism, classism, and sexism today.

18. Discuss the four reasons for the emergence of the primacy of story in biblical criticism. How does the new development in literary criticism affect your understanding of the Bible? Explain.

19. How does the distinction and relation between primary and secondary language afford a more synthetic view of the development of biblical criticism?

20. Has this book given you a deeper awareness of the importance of biblical criticism for communicating the Christian message today? How do you understand the authority of Scripture in your own life?

VII. SUGGESTED READINGS

Bornkamm, Guenther. *Jesus of Nazareth.* Trans. Irene & Fraser McLuskey with James M. Robinson. London: Hodder & Stoughton, 1960.

Cook, Michael L. *The Jesus of Faith: A Study in Christology.* NY: Paulist Press, 1981.

_____. "Jesus From the Other Side of History: Christology in Latin America," *Theological Studies* 44 (1983) 258–287.

Fitzmyer, Joseph A. *A Christological Catechism: New Testament Answers.* NY: Paulist Press, 1982.

Greeley, Andrew M. *The Jesus Myth: New Insights into the Person and Message of Jesus.* NY: Doubleday Image, 1973.

Harvey, Van A. *The Historian and the Believer: A Confrontation Between the Modern Historian's Principles of Judgment and the Christian's Will-To-Believe.* Toronto: Macmillan, 1966. Reissued: Philadelphia: The Westminster Press, 1984.

Hellwig, Monika K. *Jesus, the Compassion of God: New Perspectives on the Tradition of Christianity.* Wilmington: Michael Glazier, Inc., 1983.

Keck, Leander E. *A Future For the Historical Jesus: The Place of Jesus in Preaching and Theology.* Nashville: Abingdon Press, 1971.

Nolan, Albert. *Jesus Before Christianity.* Maryknoll: Orbis Press, 1978.

Perrin, Norman. *Rediscovering the Teaching of Jesus.* NY: Harper & Row, 1967.

Sobrino, Jon. *Christology at the Crossroads: A Latin American Approach.* Trans. John Drury. Maryknoll: Orbis Press, 1978.

Thompson, William M. *The Jesus Debate: A Survey and Synthesis.* NY: Paulist Press, 1985.

ADDITIONAL WORKS CITED

Beardslee, William A. *Literary Criticism of the New Testament.* Philadelphia: Fortress Press, 1970.

Braun, Herbert. "The Meaning of New Testament Christology." Trans. Paul J. Achtemeier in *God and Christ: Existence and Province* (ed. Robert W. Funk). NY: Harper & Row, 1968.

Bultmann, Rudolf. *Jesus and the Word.* Trans. L. P. Smith & E. H. Lantero. NY: Scribner's, 1958.

_____. "The Primitive Christian Kerygma and the Historical Jesus." Trans. & ed. by Carl E. Braaten & Roy A. Harrisville in *The Historical Jesus and the Kerygmatic Christ.* Nashville: Abingdon Press, 1964. This and its earlier (1962) companion volume *Kerygma and History* contain a number of scholarly articles on Bultmann's theology.

Conzelmann, Hans. *Jesus.* Trans. J. Raymond Lord & ed. John Reumann. Philadelphia: Fortress Press, 1973.

Crossan, John Dominic. *The Dark Interval: Towards A Theology of Story.* Niles, Illinois: Argus Communications, 1975.

Ebeling, Gerhard. *Word and Faith.* Trans. James W. Leitch. Philadelphia: Fortress Press, 1963.

_____. *Theology and Proclamation: A Discussion with Rudolf Bultmann.* Trans. John Riches. Philadelphia: Fortress Press, 1966.

Fuchs, Ernst. *Studies of the Historical Jesus.* Trans. Andrew Scobie. London: SCM Press, 1964.

Haight, Roger. *An Alternative Vision: An Interpretation of Liberation Theology.* NY: Paulist Press, 1985.

Jeremias, Joachim. *The Problem of the Historical Jesus.*
Trans. Norman Perrin. Philadelphia: Fortress Press,
1964.

_____. *New Testament Theology: The Proclamation of
Jesus.* Trans. John Bowden. NY: Scribner's, 1971.

Kaesemann, Ernst. *Essays on New Testament Themes.*
Trans. W. J. Montague. London: SCM Press, 1964.

McFague, Sallie. *Metaphorical Theology: Models of God
in Religious Language.* Philadelphia: Fortress Press,
1982.

Robinson, James M. *A New Quest of the Historical Jesus.*
London: SCM Press, 1959.

_____. "The Recent Debate on the 'New Quest'," *Journal of Biblical Religion* 30 (1962) 198–208.

Schüssler-Fiorenza, Elisabeth. *In Memory of Her: A
Feminist Theological Reconstruction of Christian Origins.* NY: Crossroad, 1984.

Schweitzer, Albert. *The Quest of the Historical Jesus.*
Trans. W. Montgomery. London: A. & C. Black, 1954.
Reissued: NY: Macmillan, 1961.

Tilley, Terrence W. *Story Theology.* Wilmington: Michael
Glazier, Inc., 1985.

BIBLICAL CITATIONS

All direct biblical quotations are taken from *The New Oxford Annotated Bible with the Apocrypha. Revised Standard Version.* Ed. Herbert G. May & Bruce M. Metzger. NY: Oxford University Press, Inc., 1973, 1977.